Canadian Baptists and Christian Higher Education

EDITED BY

G.A. RAWLYK

McGill-Queen's University Press
Kingston and Montreal

© McGill-Queen's University Press 1988
ISBN 0-7735-0677-2 (cloth)
ISBN 0-7735-0684-5 (paper)

Legal deposit third quarter 1988
Bibliothèque nationale du Québec

Printed in Canada on acid-free paper

The publication of this book is being supported
financially by a generous grant from Acadia University.

Canadian Cataloguing in Publication Data

Main entry under title:
Canadian Baptists and Christian higher education
Includes bibliographical references and index.
ISBN: 0-7735-0677-2 (bound) –
ISBN: 0-7735-0684-5 (pbk.)
1. Baptists–Education–Canada–History.
2. Church colleges–Canada–History.
I. Rawlyk, George A., 1935–   .
BX6251.C36 1988   377′.86171   C88-090269-8

Canadian Baptists and
Christian Higher Education

The ongoing debate concerning the importance of Christian higher education has significantly shaped the Canadian Baptist experience for almost two centuries and continues to do so even in the 1980s. *Canadian Baptists and Christian Higher Education* deals with this debate and its effects on three important educational institutions: Acadia University, McMaster University, and Brandon College.

Barry Moody argues that Acadia has been surprisingly open to a variety of theologies and pedagogical perspectives. His study helps explain the remarkable strength of the Baptist tradition in late nineteenth-century Nova Scotia. J.R.C. Perkin shows Watson Kirkconnell as representative of this tradition and its strength.

G.A. Rawlyk examines some of the underlying forces which significantly affected the development of McMaster University. He suggests that the cutting edge of McMaster's nineteenth-century Evangelicalism may have been dulled by the enthusiastic manner in which "consumerism" and "modernity" were appropriated by the Baptist Convention leadership which controlled the university.

Walter Ellis maintains that Brandon failed as a Baptist institution of higher learning largely because it was out of touch with Western realities. If it had been a Bible college rather than a Manitoba variant of McMaster, a Baptist Brandon might still be in existence and Convention Baptists might as a result be a far stronger force in the Canadian West.

These essays on individual institutions highlight the pressure on denominational universities to emphasize not Christian spirituality but largely secular scholarship. They will be of interest to all those who are concerned with the place of Christian higher education within not only the Baptist denomination but the entire Christian church in Canada.

G.A. Rawlyk is a member of the Department of History at Queen's University and during the 1987–88 academic year was holder of the Winthrop Picard Bell chair at Mount Allison University.

Contents

G . A .   R A W L Y K

Introduction

Since the late eighteenth century, many Canadian Baptists have had sharply divergent views of the efficacy of higher education. For some, higher education has been viewed as the worldly means whereby pristine evangelical piety is savagely undermined. And for others, higher education — as one Baptist educator put it in 1883 — was the only way true evangelicals could effectively "meet the polished shafts of a refined and subtle infidelity."[1] The ongoing Baptist debate concerning Christian higher education has significantly shaped the contours of the Canadian Baptist experience for almost two centuries. And it continues to do so even in the 1980s.

The following four chapters deal with rather different approaches to the problem of Canadian Baptists and Christian higher education. The issue is examined in an empathetic yet critical manner, and focuses on developments in the nineteenth and twentieth centuries in the maritimes, central Canada, and the west. These chapters were first presented as the Hayward Lectures at Acadia University, as part of the 1987 Baptist Heritage Conference. This conference was organized to celebrate the sesquicentennial of Acadia University and the centennial of McMaster University, as well as the twentieth anniversary of Acadia Divinity College.

In chapter 1, Professor Barry Moody of the History Department, Acadia University, presents a most interesting picture of Acadia during its first half century of existence. According to Moody, Acadia was surprisingly open to a variety of theologies and pedagogical perspectives and this he traces to the liberality and what he calls the "breadth of vision" of the Nova Scotia Baptists. In his revisionist study, Moody, among other things, helps to explain the remarkable strength of the Baptist tradition in late nineteenth century Nova Scotia.

In chapter 2, I try to understand some of the underlying forces which converged in the late nineteenth and early twentieth centuries to affect significantly the formative period of McMaster's existence. Using insights from the work of Jackson Lears and Antonio Gramsci, I suggest that McMaster's nineteenth century evangelical cutting edge may have been dulled by, among other things, the enthusiastic manner with which "consumerism" and "modernity" were appropriated by the Baptist Convention leadership which controlled the university.

Chapter 3 is written by Dr Walter E. Ellis, minister at Fairview Baptist Church, Vancouver. An accomplished historian, Ellis suggests that Brandon failed as a Baptist institution of higher learning largely because it was out of touch with western realities. If it had been a bible college rather than a Manitoba variant of McMaster University, it might still be in existence today and, furthermore, the Convention Baptists might as a result be a far stronger force in the Canadian west than they presently are.

In the final chapter, the president of Acadia University, Dr J.R.C. Perkin, deals with certain aspects of the academic career of one of his predecessors. According to Perkin, Kirkconnell made important contributions in three areas of Canadian life — multiculturalism, the Humanities Research Council of Canada, and higher education in Nova Scotia. The implicit suggestion in Perkin's chapter — one that is enlarged upon in Kirkconnell's autobiography, *A Slice of Canada* — is that Kirkconnell's Baptist faith affected all areas of his life and his thought.

It is noteworthy that the maritime Baptist approach to Christian higher education was until the past few decades very different from that in central Canada and the west. And it was different, it may be argued, largely because since the early nineteenth century maritime Baptists had been far more open to a variety of theological viewpoints than their coreligionists elsewhere in Canada. Consequently, it is not surprising that Acadia, throughout its Baptist history, was so accommodating, so open, and so liberal — unlike McMaster and Brandon, which, in the 1920s, were sources of a major fundamentalist-modernist controversy that split the non-maritime Baptists into

warring theological factions.[2] Acadia's "breadth of mind" reflected
accurately the essential nature of maritime Baptist mainstream theology during the century following the establishment of the institution. It should be kept in mind that the theology of the maritime
Baptists, from the late eighteenth century until fairly recent times,
has always been basically syncretic, placing particular emphasis on
personal religious experience rather than on a specific orthodox
ideology. Consequently, most maritime Baptists, even in the 1920s
and 1930s, did not spend very much time or energy making fine
theological distinctions. They were very much part of a Baptist tradition — stretching back to the late eighteenth century — that had
always placed more stress on "promoting a good Work" than upon
theological "Principles."[3] For maritime Baptists, therefore, even during the years of bitter fundamentalist-modernist controversy, con-
tinuity was far more appealing than abrupt change, as was a certain
degree of liberal openness at a time when an almost paranoid and
foreign fundamentalistic restrictiveness held sway elsewhere.
Maritime Baptist religious practice and belief reflected the spirituality
of Henry Alline and Harris Harding rather than that of Gresham
Machen, the Princeton Presbyterian fundamentalist, or T.T. Shields,
the influential Ontario fundamentalist Baptist leader. Most maritime
Baptists in the period before the second world war could not em-
pathize with the main North American fundamentalist or modernist
propagandists because they perceived religion in a radically different
manner. In a sense, they, unlike many of their Baptist cousins in
central Canada and the west, had not, as yet, experienced the profound Americanization of their popular culture. Thus they were very
successful in the interwar years in resisting the fundamentalist-
modernist bombardment from the south, especially when the bombardment was aimed at Acadia — an institution they still regarded
as a sensitive reflector of the maritime Baptist consensus.

It is sometimes forgotten that in the 1930s T.T. Shields attempted
to split the maritime Convention as he had done the Ontario and
Quebec convention a decade earlier. He encouraged two able Baptist
fundamentalist ministers — the Reverends J.J. Sidey and J.B. Daggett
— who, at the time, were associated with Baptist churches in the
Kingston region of Nova Scotia. Sidey and Daggett attacked Acadia
as being an intellectual outpost of the University of Chicago — "the
greatest infidel factory in America."[4] Moreover, Sidey and Daggett

contended that students at Acadia were being taught by "modernist" and "unitarian" professors who openly scoffed at "the divinity of the Lord" and regarded evolution as the inspired gospel of the new scientific élite.[5] But when Daggett and Sidey and their handful of supporters attempted between 1933 and 1935 to split the Convention into a fundamentalist majority and a modernist rump, they were only able to take two and possibly three small Baptist churches, out of over 500, out of the Convention. A few others, however, experienced bitter divisions which resulted in the creation of independent Baptist churches within the Convention communities. Acadia was certainly not perceived as a McMaster or a Brandon by most members of the Maritime Baptist constituency and Sidey and Daggett only realized this after their Shields inspired and orchestrated secession movement had miserably failed.

What was particularly striking about the 1987 Hayward Lectures and the often vigorous discussion they generated were the overarching twin themes of McMaster imperialism and secularization in the various papers. From the 1880s to the 1960s, when Acadia became a kind of maritime McMaster, McMaster University certainly perceived itself as *the* premier Canadian Baptist institution of higher learning. Regarding the maritimes as a backwater of cultural, religious, economic, and political despair, those who controlled the academic fortunes of McMaster were content to see Acadia as a minor league operation loosely associated with the Toronto-Hamilton major league academic franchise. And because of the powerful sense of collective inferiority that engulfed the area in the post-Confederation period, most maritime Baptists seemed content to accept their second class status.

McMaster's real imperialistic thrust, however, before the second world war was a western, not an eastern, one — slavishly following the Upper Canadian pattern of expansion. And, consequently, Brandon College, which was founded in 1899, found itself under tremendous pressure to emulate McMaster. It was Brandon's destiny to become a prairie McMaster rather than an indigenous western institution, sensitively reflecting unique local conditions. The central thesis of Walter Ellis — that the McMaster pattern of Christian higher education was largely irrelevant for the west and seriously weakened the Baptist position west of Ontario — is certainly compelling. It seems fairly obvious that western Baptists in the late nineteenth and early twentieth centuries would have been far better off with a bible college than with a university if their hope was to make a significant impact on the religious culture of the west.

The McMaster influence over Baptist higher education in Canada continued after World War II when Acadia University itself virtually replicated the McMaster example. The principal agent for the secularization of Acadia was Watson Kirkconnell, who had always been very impressed with the McMaster experiment. During Kirkconnell's presidency, from 1948 to 1964, as President Perkin implicitly suggests in his chapter, Kirkconnell pushed Acadia in McMaster's direction, abandoning in the process the Baptist principle of the separation of church and state, as well as the nineteenth century maritime Baptist ideal of Christian higher education. Kirkconnell wanted Acadia to become the McMaster of the east, with suitable provincial funding, an excellent science program, and a theological college that would be its link with an increasingly irrelevant denominational past. In his autobiography, *A Slice of Canada*, Kirkconnell was very proud of his crucially important role in bringing about the secularization of Acadia.[6] He had led the successful counter-offensive against a growing faction in the Convention which, in 1965, was demanding "that the Acadia faculty must be made up of 'professors who have a personal belief and commitment to Jesus Christ.'"[7] As Professor Moody convincingly argues, this Kirkconnell policy was indeed an abandonment of Acadia's founding principle.

More might have been made of Kirkconnell's very important role in the so-called modernization of Acadia. Some readers of this book might argue that too much has been made of Howard Primrose Whidden's contribution to the secularization of Brandon and McMaster. In a sense, if there is a villain in this study, it is Whidden. Born in Antigonish, Nova Scotia in 1871, Whidden graduated from Acadia in 1891 and from McMaster in theology three years later. After serving a number of Baptist churches in Ontario and the United States and teaching both at McMaster and Brandon, Whidden was president of Brandon from 1912 to 1923 and chancellor of McMaster from 1923 to 1941. He died in Toronto on 30 March, 1952.[8]

When he graduated from Acadia, Whidden was a typical maritime Baptist — a person who sensitively balanced his pietism and his reason. By the time he became president of Brandon, however, the pietism seems to have been overwhelmed by his growing obsession with economic progress and liberal learning. From 1912 on, a true university for Whidden was one which placed special emphasis not on the development of Christian spirituality but on modern, relevant scholarship. He therefore spent his years at Brandon and McMaster in transforming the seemingly backward looking Christian schools into modern, secular universities. Whidden was determined to thrust those new Baptist institutions of higher learning into the mainstream of North American academic development. And in this, of course, he largely succeeded.

Whidden's academic career provides a marvelous lens through which to examine the secularization of Baptist higher education in Canada. His career encapsulates this transformation. He seemed to be on the cutting edge of Canadian progress; Whidden was also, the evidence suggests, determined to use his growing influence and power to strengthen the cultural hegemony of the new and powerful forces of economic change. Whidden was what has recently been called one of the key "point men," one of the "most educated and cosmopolitan products of an urbanizing, secularizing society" as it moved from "a Protestant to a therapeutic world view."[9]

Canadian Baptists and Christian Higher Education is not, of course, a definitive study. Rather, it is suggestive, probing, and, in places, controversial. It is hoped that the publication of the 1987 Hayward Lectures will help to trigger a sustained debate in Canada about the relevance and importance of so-called Christian higher education, not only among Baptists, but within the entire Christian Church in Canada.

Canadian Baptists and
Christian Higher Education

BARRY M. MOODY

Breadth of Vision, Breadth of Mind: The Baptists and Acadia College

On a warm August evening in 1888 in Wolfville, Nova Scotia, students, faculty, politicians and friends gathered in Assembly Hall, Acadia College, to celebrate that institution's golden jubilee. Nearly 2,000 people crowded the building in what the Halifax *Herald* called "the grandest gathering that ever took place west of Halifax."[1] The paper further enthused: "The wealth and brains, the youth and beauty, and the strength and manhood of the denomination were assembled."[2] The building was suitably decorated with plants and flowers, spruce boughs and Chinese lanterns. And mounted high on the wall was the biblical text "Hitherto the Lord hath helped us."

Having seen the sights and been suitably impressed by the decorations, the assembled guests settled down for a long program of music and speeches. That evening, and the following day, speaker after speaker rose to extol the virtues of Acadia College and praise all that had been accomplished in the past fifty years. But there was also a serious attempt on the part of those present to understand *how* it had all come about. How could one explain the survival and growth of the college when everything would seem to have worked against it?

As to the underlying cause for the success of the institution, there was no doubt in the minds of those present. It was heralded by the motto on the wall and reiterated by nearly every speaker on the program. For the Jubilee sermon, the Reverend Edward Manning Saunders, the prominent Halifax Baptist clergyman, took as his text 1 Corinthians 3:9: "For we are laborers together with God." The founding and development of Acadia College had been in accordance with the purposes of God Himself, and only in this way could maritime Baptists explain its remarkable success in the face of great opposition and hardship. Saunders argued that "The bright and dark features, the prosperity and the adversity, all alike contribute to the evidence that the beginning and work of Acadia College have been according to the good pleasure of Him under whose superintendence and by whose help the institutions [Acadia and Horton Academy] have continued till this day."[3] This not only explained the past but also gave purpose to the future. "Given the importance of the times in which we live," Saunders asked rhetorically, "should we now close Acadia? Nay verily! but let the holy purpose take, if possible, a deeper and firmer hold of the Baptist heart to make Acadia College fill to the full God's purpose, to the joy of the living, the unborn, and those who, having finished their course, are now in the presence of God."[4]

Having acknowledged God as author and director of this accomplishment, the speakers went on to probe still further in their efforts to understand the college which they so obviously loved and respected. If God was the author, what was the agency by which all this had been accomplished? The anonymous writer of the memorial address perceptively put his finger on the beginning of an important understanding of Acadia College in the nineteenth century without, perhaps, realizing the significance of what he was saying. He wrote: "Standing in 1828 we see two marvellous trains of events in progress, the one arising away back in the latter half of the last century and gathering elements of strength in ever increasing ration, the other dating visibly only a few years previous to 1828, both nearing each other, and at length culminating in that year in the founding of a Seminary of learning at Wolfville, which was shortly to grow into Acadia College."[5] It was, he argued, the power unleashed by the "Great Awakening" and its charismatic preacher Henry Alline, united with the intellectual leadership brought into the denomination by the rupture in Saint Paul's Anglican Church in Halifax in the mid-1820s, that had produced the marvellous results. God, with His human agents, thus stood at the centre of their understanding of the Acadia College of their time.

In spite of the simplicity of expression, the author did have grasp of a fundamental concept in comprehending the nature of the institution whose founding was celebrated that evening. Acadia College was the result of the coming together of not just two divergent streams, however, but of many, and any understanding of the institution in the nineteenth century must begin with an acceptance of this remarkable diversity that characterized not only its founding but also its subsequent development. It was this diversity that moulded and shaped the college and accounted for both its survival and the overwhelming success that was celebrated so joyfully and thankfully that evening in 1888. And it was that diversity of origin that gave Acadia the breadth of vision and of mind that was the hallmark of the institution in the nineteenth century.

When one examines the founding of Canada's universities in the first half of the last century, it is quickly apparent that, for most of them, the driving force, the leadership, and the ideas came from a small but significant element. Such leadership was usually British-born, steeped in the traditions of its particular religious heritage, drawn from the upper or upper-middle classes, and with considerable exposure to and familiarity with the educational philosophy of its time and place. The educational leaders of the Anglican, or Presbyterian, or Roman Catholic churches moved decisively to found institutions that reflected their views and fulfilled their needs. Such colleges as McGill in Montreal, King's in Windsor, or Queen's in Kingston were also the product of years of debate and careful planning to ensure that the institution thus built would be an accurate reflection of the views of the elite, social or religious, that undertook that building. There certainly was not always unanimity among such builders — in fact, there seldom was. However, the differences, the disagreements, the quarrels over philosophy or program usually took place within carefully defined limits, limits imposed by the thinking of that religious or social elite.[6]

The dissenting tradition in Canada, however, has a very different development, leading in very different directions. Acadia University is the product of that dissenting tradition, and nothing marks the early development of this institution as clearly or as forcefully as does the diversity and the complexity of that tradition. Acadia was founded by the Baptists of Nova Scotia and developed by the Baptists of the maritime provinces — in the nineteenth century an amorphous, divergent, and often acrimonious body that almost defies definition. Within the bounds of that denomination one could find almost every conceivable tradition, philosophy, belief, and aspiration, existing in often uneasy relationship one with another. A careful study of the Baptist denomination in the nineteenth century, and of Acadia University, leads to the conclusion that the Baptists *as a body* were a most undogmatic people. That many individual Baptists held very strong and well-developed religious ideas is not to be doubted for a moment, but to argue that these were understood or accepted by the majority of their fellow Baptists cannot be maintained. In the nineteenth century, the Baptist denomination was just taking shape in the maritime colonies and, beyond a few fundamentals such as the central importance of regeneration and adult baptism by immersion, there was little unity of agreement. Many key questions had not yet even been asked, let alone answered, by the denomination as a whole. Whatever changes might take place by the end of the last century or in the early decades of the twentieth century, and however dogmatic the denomination might later become, it must be remembered that Acadia University was not founded, as was McMaster, in the 1880s, or in the early twentieth century, but in 1838, when the denomination, and therefore its creation — the college — were dominated by very different and very divergent ideas. It is perhaps this that has so perplexed, and at times infuriated, some maritime Baptists about "their" university in this century.

Some understanding of the diversity of the denomination and of the college itself can perhaps be gained by a quick look at the men who occupied the stage at Acadia's first graduating exercises — the annual anniversary services, as they were called. That date was 16 June 1843, and it was an especially proud day for many Nova Scotia Baptists for the first fruits of their academic labours were now to be reaped. The platform party that day was composed of the Honourable Charles Ramage Prescott, Thomas Andrew Strange DeWolfe, the Honourable J.W. Johnston (the attorney general), Simon Fitch, Charles Harris, and Caleb Bill (governors of the college), the Reverend Edmund A. Crawley, the Reverend John Pryor, and Isaac Chipman (professors), and the Reverends Theodore Seth Harding and Edward Manning. In terms of age, education, background, views, and philosophies, one could hardly have assembled a more dissimilar group, and yet there they were, applauding the four young men who that day comprised Acadia's first graduating class.[7]

Prescott, from nearby Starr's Point, and DeWolfe, from Wolfville itself, were both Nova Scotia government appointees to the Board of Governors under the terms of the recently approved college charter. Prescott was a well-known orchardist and former member of the Legislative Council. DeWolfe was a prominent merchant, member of the Legislative Assembly for Kings County, and member of the executive council. Both were Anglicans.[8]

Simon Fitch, Charles Harris, and Caleb Bill were Baptists, of New England Planter descent. Bill was the brother of the Reverend I.E. Bill, who played a prominent part in the founding of Acadia and was one of its strongest supporters. Caleb Bill would later serve as MLA for Kings County and, after Confederation, was one of Nova Scotia's representatives in the Canadian Senate. Fitch would serve Acadia long and loyally, both on the board and as a fund raiser.[9]

The Honourable J.W. Johnston, the attorney general of the colony, was of far greater significance to Acadia than these other five men combined. Born in Jamaica of loyalist parents, Johnston was trained in the law and quickly became a prominent lawyer in Halifax, and a leading member of Saint Paul's Anglican Church in that city. In the mid-1820s a major quarrel with Bishop John Inglis over the appointment of a suitable evangelical minister led to the embittered departure from the Anglican Church of Johnston and a number of other dissidents. After considerable hesitation and uncertainty, Johnston became a member of Granville Street Baptist Church in Halifax and played a leading role in the denomination for the rest of his life. His own involvement in politics as a Conservative, and in particular his antipathy to the Reformer, Joseph Howe, would eventually drag the Baptists into the worst political quarrel in which they ever involved themselves. However, Johnston's political position had served the Baptists well in their search for support for Acadia's charter and for provincial funding. Johnston had been one of the driving forces behind the founding of the institution and was one of her stalwart supporters, provided, of course, that things went as Johnston wanted. Johnston — moderate Tory, former Anglican, Haligonian — could sit on that platform with confidence and pride, never perhaps realizing the gulf that still separated him from many of the Baptists in the audience.[10]

The three professors assembled there that day also represent a study in contrast. Edmund A. Crawley, John Pryor, and Isaac Chipman constituted the entire teaching staff of Acadia College in 1843. But even in such small numbers they represented a wider range of background and philosophies than was to be found at most of the other British North American universities of the time.

Crawley and Pryor shared much in common, and stood together on many issues. A native of England, Crawley was raised in Cape Breton, while Pryor was born and reared in Halifax. Of well-to-do, upper class families, both were brought up in the Anglican Church and both attended King's College, Windsor, where they came under strong evangelical influences. Along with Johnston, and others, both were involved in the rupture in Saint Paul's and were part of the move to the Baptist position that followed. Crawley had been one of the key men in the establishment of Horton Academy in 1828, and Pryor became its second principal in 1830. Both men studied theology in the United States and both had become ordained Baptist ministers. They were also alike in that they continued to rely for their power in the denomination on the influential Halifax Baptist clique composed of former Anglicans. Pryor and Crawley would each become president of the institution they had helped to found, and around both would swirl storms of controversy for much of their lives.[11]

The much younger Isaac Chipman was very different from his colleagues. Born in the Annapolis Valley only a few miles from Horton, the son of a proud Planter family, Chipman had been raised in a pious Baptist home and sent to the newly established Horton Academy for his education. A brilliant student and devout Christian, young Chipman considered a career in the ministry before turning to teaching. He received his college education at Waterville College, Maine, and returned to Nova Scotia shortly after the founding of Acadia College. He gave the rest of his life to university teaching at a time when it was usual in British North America for only ordained ministers to hold such positions. The survival and growth of Acadia in the 1840s and early 50s was in no small measure due to Chipman's energy, foresight, and self-sacrifice.[12]

The two aged ministers who also occupied a proud place on the platform that memorable day were numbered among the "Fathers" of the denomination. Both men were in their seventies, and each represented long years of service to the Baptist cause. Harding, who would so eloquently invoke God's blessings on the day's proceedings, had served for nearly fifty years as the minister of the Horton Baptist Church. Of Planter stock, with no formal education of which to boast, he had begun his ministry as a Methodist preacher and on a number of occasions his commitment to the Baptist cause would temporarily weaken. Beside him sat the aged Edward Manning, pastor of the Cornwallis Baptist Church, and probably the most respected minister in the denomination. Yet he too showed signs of a non-Baptist beginning. Born in Ireland, into a Roman Catholic family, Manning had been converted in Nova Scotia in the aftermath of the Great Awakening, had become a New Light Congregationalist, and then, by slow steps, a Baptist. Convinced of the necessity of formal education, he had aided materially in the movement to found Horton Academy in 1828 and Acadia College in 1838, and had served as the chairman of the Nova Scotia Baptist Education Society since its inception. And now he sat on the platform and presided over Acadia's first graduation exercises, a man with little formal schooling himself.[13]

Even a superficial glance at this diverse assemblage on the Acadia platform speaks volumes as to the origins of this institution. In terms of background, religious upbringing, educational attainments, and philosophies, it would be difficult to assemble a more disparate group at any college in Canada at that time. And when one looks below the surface, the range and the complexity of those who founded and directed Acadia become even more striking. In fact, aside from a few essentials, there appeared to be little unanimity; nor, in fact, was such unanimity expected. Unlike most colleges founded in Canada at this time, Acadia was not established to promote a specific ideology or dogma, for the Baptists of Nova Scotia did not collectively possess one. It was not built to conserve a way of life, but to be the vehicle by which that life could be changed. It existed not to safeguard a social position, but to advance it. Drawing on such a diverse background, Acadia would be broadly based and remarkably tolerant of dissenting views. In this lay the real strength of the college in the nineteenth century.

Those men sitting on that platform in 1843 represented not only the superficial differences alluded to, but were symbolic of far more significant streams that had come together to create the Baptist denomination and its child, Acadia College. It was Acadia's good fortune to have been founded at a time when there was a healthy, invigorating tension between the forces of town and country, the educated and the uneducated, the upper class and the "middling sort." The college that these different forces created was not a compromise, a *via media*, but rather an exciting combination of at times contradictory ideas and aspirations.

Certainly, such divergence was observable in the founding itself. Acadia was established to serve a number of ends, to accomplish a variety of purposes, to hew out more than one new path. It is often assumed that the chief purpose of the new institution was to produce more ministers to spread over the land, adding converts to the Baptist churches. The denomination, however, was too deeply divided over the issue of an educated clergy to accept this as the rationale for the new college's existence. For the rest of the century and, it could be argued, beyond, many maritime Baptists harboured considerable fear that education would smother piety, that the search for earthly wisdom would divert the pious young man from his search for the real meaning of life. For more than sixty years after Acadia's founding, theology would be taught only intermittently, largely because the Baptist churches of the maritimes would not give sufficient money to support such a program.[14] Part of this reluctance perhaps stems from the fact that, collectively, maritime Baptists had not yet decided what their theology really was. No, if Baptists had waited until they were ready to found a theological institution, there would have been no new Baptist college in 1838, and perhaps not in that century.

Nor could the Baptists agree on who should control a college, or what constituency it should serve. A scant two months before he would lead the Baptists in the founding of Acadia College on 15 November 1838, Edmund Crawley still confidently opposed such a move, expecting a professorship at a newly reconstituted Dalhousie. For at least three of those men on the platform in 1843 — Crawley, Pryor, and Johnston — there was clearly no fear of a state controlled college, located in the heart of downtown Halifax. And yet it was just such fears that had prevented many of the rural Baptists from supporting the attempts to open Dalhousie College at last — fear of state dominated education and distaste for all that "city life" stood for.[15] Beyond that, there was a deep cleavage within the denomination concerning *who* should receive an education. Pervading many of the petitions, the letters to the editor, and the speeches of the next few years was the underlying conviction that education ought to be placed within the reach of every one, by which they meant, of course, within the reach of every male. There was strong opposition to the idea of education for an elite only, whether that elite was a social or an intellectual one. Education for the common people, and the ordinary intellect, thus becomes an important underlying theme in Acadia's early development, one that ought not to be overlooked in placing this institution in the broader context of nineteenth-century Canadian higher education.[16] Given the background from which they came, and the positions they continued to occupy, it is not surprising to find that some of the Halifax Baptists should reveal a fair amount of ambivalence on this subject.[17]

If there was no unanimity as to who should be taught, or under what direction, there was considerably less certainty as to *what* should be taught. In fact, there was remarkably little concern expressed over this matter during Acadia's first fifty years. One searches the newspapers, Convention reports and even the minutes of the Board of Governors almost in vain for a serious discussion as to what constituted a proper education at a Baptist-controlled college. Occasionally one finds reference to the need for adding certain courses to the curriculum, such as modern languages or various branches of science, but almost invariably the ensuing discussion centred on the cost, not the appropriateness, of the proposed addition.[18] Even theological education seldom roused nineteenth-century maritime Baptists to debate. Once again, it was usually the cost rather than the subject matter that provoked discussion. Usually less than one-third of the Nova Scotia, Prince Edward Island, and New Brunswick Baptist churches sent in their expected donations to fund the chair of theology.[19] Even the furious debate in the early 1880s over the establishment of the chair of didactics and education appears to have had much more to do with Baptist politics and personalities than with pedagogical principles.[20] The Convention, and maritime Baptists in general, seemed content to leave matters of program, about which they knew little, in the hands of the president and faculty of the college. In the twentieth century, they were no longer content always to do so, nor did they always reveal the same confidence in the college and its staff.[21]

None of this is to suggest that the nineteenth-century Baptists who did concern themselves with higher education — by no means always the majority of the denomination — did not have a firm and generally accepted idea of what their college actually should accomplish. With the possible exception of the Halifax clique — and their views changed so quickly and conveniently that it is often hard to pin them down — there seems to have been a basic unifying theme running through much of the discussion concerning higher education during this half century. Certainly it was expected that Acadia would be a Christian college, and that point is reiterated time after time in the years after its founding. It underlay the aversion to and rejection of Dalhousie College or any other government-controlled institution of higher learning. Their college, and the education received there, was to be God centred; of that there could be no doubt. However, their means of achieving this end was not to be found primarily in control of the curriculum, but in the careful development of the very atmosphere of the institution.

From the beginning, the founders of Acadia and those who backed them rejected the idea of a narrow sectarian base for the college. Given the difficulty inherent in deciding what was uniquely and distinctly "Baptist" at this time, it is perhaps less surprising than it might be to see a broad "Christian" base being chosen. As a result there was in the original charter that phrase of which successive generations would be so proud:

And be it further enacted, That no Religious Tests or subscriptions shall be required of the Professors, Fellows, Scholars, Graduates, Students or Officers of the said College; but that all the privileges and advantages thereof shall be open and free to all and every Person and Persons whomsoever, without regard to Religious persuasion;[22]

At times, it should be noted, too much has been read into that clause and totally incorrect construction placed upon it.[23] The rest of that paragraph and many other pronouncements of the nineteenth century make it abundantly clear that where "Religious" was written "Denominational" was actually meant. The founders were certainly broad minded for the times, but it would be quite wrong to believe that they contemplated for a moment the idea of a non-Christian teaching at Acadia. That would have defeated one of the main purposes in establishing the institution. The second half of the above clause, usually omitted in any discussion of this issue, makes the intention much clearer. It reads:

and it shall and may be lawful for the Trustees and Governors of the said College to select as Professors, and other Teachers or Officers, competent persons of any Religious persuasion whatever, provided such Person or Persons shall be of moral and religious character.

A memorandum drawn up in early 1839 further clarifies the thinking of the founders on this important subject. It reads in part: "any competent person possessed of vital piety and good moral character shall be eligible to a professor's chair without regard to his religious denomination."[24] And here one is getting close to the heart of the concept of "Christian education" as understood and practised by the founders and supporters of Acadia College in the nineteenth century. It was in the Christian character of the professors and the Christian character of the institution itself, not in the content of the courses or the selection of the curriculum, that these Baptists placed their reliance. And for the rest of the century the ultimate success of Acadia College would be measured not in the Cicero memorized or the theorems learned but in the souls won for Christ. The successive religious revivals that swept the campus were clear proof of God's seal of approval, that Acadia was "so evidently owned and blessed of God," as one writer phrased it.[25] Writing many years later about the founding, John Pryor recorded that "our Baptist friends had a strong prejudice against education, as they feared it would injure the young, 'teaching them philosophy & vain conceit.' This prejudice wore off, when it pleased the Lord to bless us with revival after revival, so that as dear Father Manning used to say 'the Academy instead of being an ice-house to freeze out religion, had become a very hot-bed of piety.'"[26] In 1863, the president, J.M. Cramp, wrote to the *Christian Messenger*: "We greatly need the baptism of the Spirit here. In other respects our prospects were never more favourable. But oh that God would come, in the might and majesty of his grace, to call the dead to life."[27] In 1874, that same newspaper carried an article entitled "The Presence of Christ at Acadia" which showed how deeply entrenched the Acadia revivalist tradition had become: "The present Senior class had considerable apprehension lest they should leave the College without seeing the work of God revive. They, with the other students of both departments, prayed and wrestled and worked; and the Lord, at last, made bare His arm to save."[28] Thirty students were converted in the ensuing revival.

The feelings of many Baptists were well summed up in the letter to the editor of one writer commenting on the meaning of this revival.

If any doubt existed as to the propriety of keeping up a separate *denominational* College, surely that doubt will now give way to faith. In what other way could this priceless blessing to our sons and daughters have been secured? They have received the best of all educational attainments, for the "fear of the Lord is the beginning of wisdom." … In what University, of a general and mixed nature, would our children have reaped these religious beliefs? Where do we ever read of religious revival at a National or Provincial University? It is one of the most striking facts in connection with the history of Acadia College that not once or twice, but many times powerful and far reaching manifestations of Divine grace have been experienced within her walls.[29]

What one profoundly experienced in the core of one's being, not what one learned rationally in the classroom, was the essence of the Acadia idea of a "Christian education." It was the providing of the necessary Christian atmosphere and Christian leadership, not the selection of a carefully regulated curriculum, that was perceived to be the main responsibility of the governors and professors of Acadia. Acting upon that belief gave the college very important freedom in course selection and program planning in the nineteenth century.[30]

If maritime Baptists of the last century were deeply divided over many aspects of higher education, there was, nonetheless, widespread agreement in their assessment of the times in which they lived. The feeling that they lived in an age of progress, a time of general advancement, seems to have pervaded their society. Everywhere they looked in the middle decades of that century they saw "The Progressive March of Human History," as one speaker entitled his lecture to the Acadia Athenaeum Society.[31] What was very clear was that if they did not go forward, both as individuals and as a denomination, they would go backward. And that they were not prepared to do. Not only was there general and observable upward movement in their society, but clearly the Baptist cause in the maritime colonies in the first half of the century was also on the rise. From very small beginnings it had mushroomed by mid-century into one of the most dynamic of the maritime denominations.[32] It had spread throughout the countryside in all three colonies, leading to the founding of dozens of new churches in that period. Moreover, several of the leaders saw something very significant in the dramatic inroads made in the 1820s into the upper classes of Halifax and Saint John, surely clear proof of God's work on the march.[33]

The growing conviction that education held the key to advancement proved a powerful stimulus to the establishment of Horton Academy and then Acadia College.[34] And it certainly provided the glue which bound disparate elements within the denomination together in their support of the institutions. The opposition to the granting of Acadia's charter,[35] Joseph Howe's attacks on the college in the 1840s (because of Baptist support for his archrival, Johnston),[36] and the problems over provincial support were all seen by many Baptists as part of a plot to deprive them of the means of advancement, to keep them in subservient positions forever. Writing to the newspaper in 1843, one female correspondent noted:

Our enemies in Nova Scotia have ever derided the Baptists for their want of learning, and now they are trying to cut off the only means through which they can obtain it ... I have many years longed to see the day when grace, good sense, native talent and learning, should be united, and more generally enjoyed by the Baptists in N. Scotia, and at the age of sixty-six, I have seen that day begin to dawn.[37]

An editorial a decade and a half later, in recommending Horton Academy to its readers, observed:

The demand for education by all classes cannot fail to make this and other similar institutions more and more highly valued, as we proceed in the onward march of improvement. A larger amount of educational training is required now to enable a young man to maintain his position than formerly, and unless his early years are improved by the diligent use of all his opportunities, he will soon find himself left behind by those perhaps with fewer advantages but who have been early trained to habits of industry... Those able to give their sons such a course of training would benefit them more by an expenditure of five pounds in this way, than by neglecting their education and leaving them in possession of hundreds or thousands.[38]

Colleges were, it was maintained later, "the very fountains of civilization, and safeguards from a return to primitive ignorance."[39] Of course, there were many Baptists who feared, not admired, institutions of higher education. But among those who did support education, whether upper-class, former Anglicans from Halifax, or rural Baptist farmers from Annapolis County or the upper Saint John River Valley, there seemed to be general agreement that an institution of higher learning, under Baptist sponsorship, offered them the best means by which the general advancement of the denomination and of their sons and grandsons could be secured. As the editor of the Baptist press wrote in 1841, it would soon be apparent "whether the Baptists as a Denomination are hereafter to appeal to others than those of their own body, to advocate their claims before the public, in the Halls of our Legislature, in our Courts of Justice, and in conducting the operations of the Press — in truth, whether in all the leading and important matters that regard the welfare of society, they are to become the hewers of wood and drawers of water, to those who shall have assumed a merited superiority over them."[40] It was the utilitarian aspects of education, then, that attracted these people, and they would demand of Acadia a useful, practical course of training for the aspiring generations to come. The search for "useful" education to aid in their general advancement would see the exploration of many new fields by Acadia's directors over the first sixty years.

The type and quality of the men that Acadia would attract as professors and presidents during that period is the final factor that should be looked at in assessing the origins of Acadia's approach to education. In looking at the four men who presided over Acadia until near the end of the century, one thing becomes abundantly clear. Although each was a strong, forceful individual, with well-developed ideas and concepts of his own, none was able so completely to dominate the institution as to alter fundamentally its direction. For better or worse, Acadia during this period had no J.W. Dawson of McGill or G.M. Grant of Queen's, no one in whose life and thoughts may be seen the essence of the college.[41]

During the first crucial years there was no president at all, with the college totally in the hands of the faculty. John Pryor's presidency (1847-50) was brief and unimaginative, and the later scandals involving sexual and financial indiscretions which rocked his ministry destroyed his influence both at Acadia and within the denomination.[42] John Mockett Cramp was very different from Pryor, the former Anglican and Haligonian. English born and trained in the dissenting college tradition of England, Cramp brought to Acadia yet another set of educational ideas. He was also an outstanding scholar, and served Acadia as president, teacher, and friend for three decades (1851-81). He clearly had the intellect and the rigorous commitment to have imposed his ideas and his philosophies on the still-malleable institution. However, Cramp did not possess the necessary desire to so control the college, nor did he get the opportunity.[43] The determination of the Halifax clique to once again seize control of Acadia in the early 1850s, and their manipulation of the situation and of Cramp, resulted in the latter being rather ruthlessly, if temporarily, shouldered aside and replaced by the more aggressive Edmund Crawley.[44]

Certainly in Crawley Acadia had a president with sufficient determination and willpower to play the part of a Dawson or Grant. Two things only did he lack. One was sufficient time to carry out any such plan; the other was the necessary intellect for the job. If one is looking in Acadia's history for evidence of providential intervention, surely one might begin by a glance at the chain of events which led to the sudden departure in the mid-1850s of Edmund Crawley, following his investing one-third of Acadia's endowment fund in a highly speculative American mining venture that quickly went bankrupt. Crawley's short and troubled presidency (1853-56) was a disaster for the college. Although because of his Halifax connections he would prove remarkably durable and continue to exert considerable influence over Acadia's development, it was, thankfully, never the all-pervading control that he had once striven to achieve.[45]

Acadia's fourth president, A.W. Sawyer, brought yet another major influence to the campus, or rather reinforced one already present. Sawyer was American born and American trained, and unlike all of his predecessors, had considerable experience in college teaching and administration before coming to Acadia as president. Sawyer served the college from 1869 to 1896, thus having ample time to mould and shape, and certainly he did this to a considerable degree. Acadia was greatly influenced by Sawyer's long regime, but he never attempted to so control or alter the institution's character as to remake it in his own image. Perhaps after thirty years of rather rugged survival it was already too late for one personality to alter significantly Acadia's course.[46]

Taking the four presidents together, it is clear that Acadia during this time was the beneficiary of remarkably wide-ranging views and talents. Few universities in Canada in the nineteenth century proved themselves as prepared to borrow so heavily or willingly from such a combination of native, American, and English talent and tradition. Much the same flexibility and breadth is observable when one looks at the faculty employed during this period.

The basis of the Acadia approach to faculty was revealed in the clause of the charter referred to earlier. Unlike so many other institutions of higher education in Canada, an exclusivist hiring policy was never pursued at Acadia. An examination of the religious affiliation of professors and teachers at the college and academy in the nineteenth century makes it very clear that more than lip service was being paid to the declaration of religious freedom. A man's broader moral and religious convictions were more important to his prospective employer than any narrow denominational label. Thus, for example, in the late 1850s Acadia could have the stimulating experience of having on campus, as its first professor of French and German, Gustave Peple, a Belgian educated by the Moravians in Europe.[47] Rather than drawing narrowly on only one aspect of the Christian Church, as it was still quite common to do in higher education circles in Canada, Acadia was prepared to cast a wider net. Even with its refusal to move outside the boundaries of evangelical Christianity, the college still possessed a broader faculty base than many of her sister institutions.[48]

One other aspect of policy concerning faculty, or rather potential faculty, ought to be mentioned. Lacking slavish attachments to religious bodies or educational institutions in either the mother country or the United States, and with very real pride in their college, the Baptist denomination and the Board of Governors of Acadia expressed no reservations about hiring Acadia's own sons. In this Acadia was one of the first truly "Canadian" colleges, unafraid and unashamed of native British North Americans at a time when so many felt that unless one possessed an Oxford, Cambridge, or Edinburgh degree (or, at the very least, one from Harvard or Yale), then one was not truly educated. Acadia's first two faculty members, Pryor and Crawley, both had their degrees from a Nova Scotia college, King's in Windsor. The third professor, added in 1840, was Isaac Chipman, a native of the Annapolis Valley, a graduate of Horton Academy and an American college. The financial and career sacrifices that Chipman made for the institution, the burdens that he carried, and the brilliance of his mind and the piety of his life would thereafter have made it impossible for aspersions to be cast on anyone merely because he was native-born or educated in Wolfville.[49] A healthy respect was certainly maintained for the great universities of the age, and many a young Acadia graduate was sent off for further study at an Edinburgh or a Harvard, but a healthy respect was accorded their own institution as well. No sign of a "colonial mentality" is observable here. By 1863 the *Christian Messenger* could enthuse: "It is a very gratifying circumstance that Acadia College will not henceforth be dependent on other countries for Professors. Her chairs will be filled by her own sons. The list of graduates contains the names of gentlemen who are well qualified to take any position which their Alma Mater may assign them."[50] Acadia by no means hired solely her own in the nineteenth century, but she was clearly unafraid of seeing a native-born, native-trained faculty at a Canadian college.

Acadia's comparatively liberal hiring practices brought to the campus men of diverse backgrounds, training, and ideas, certainly adding to the complexity and strength of the institution. It could be argued that even the willingness to hire her native sons added substantially to the breadth of the institution. Most of these Acadia graduates studied at other institutions before returning to their alma mater to teach, bringing with them, of course, a wide range of views and experiences. Does the fact that these men were not strangers, that they were familiar faces and trusted intellects, help explain the apparent ease with which such professors slipped into the life of the university, and the denomination, with few questions asked about their views either by the governors or the denomination as a whole? Both A.B. McKillop and Ramsay Cook, in their books on critical inquiry and social criticism in Victorian Canada, have pointed out the extensive suspicion, even fear, of German ideas and German universities that pervaded much of Canada in the latter half of the nineteenth century, and the tension that it caused in some Canadian universities.[51] Yet, in 1878 Daniel Morse Welton, Acadia class of 1855, latterly pastor of the Baptist Church in Windsor, took a Ph.D. at the University of Leipzig, and then returned to his theology professorship at Acadia College. Far from fearing such new influences, Acadia gave Welton an honorary Doctorate of Divinity in 1884.[52] Was Welton more acceptable, more trusted, within the Acadia and Baptist community because he was one of their own, not a stranger arriving with new and perhaps dangerous ideas? Did new concepts and ways of thinking thus find an easier entry into the college system because of such familiarity with the man, if not the subject matter? Certainly Welton was not the only such graduate to return to his alma mater bearing strange gifts from abroad.

As important as it is to examine who was hired to teach at Acadia and why, it is perhaps of equal significance to see who was not hired by the college in the nineteenth century. Within the bounds of Protestant Christianity, there was one notable element largely lacking from the Acadia faculty and the Acadia experience, and this absence does much to distinguish this college from most other nineteenth-century English-Canadian institutions. McKillop has written that in the last century "Canadian education was shaped by men who were trained at Scottish universities."[53] Almost everywhere one looks in English Canada one sees the validity of such a statement — almost everywhere, but not at Acadia. Since it had few faculty members and no administrators trained at the great Scottish universities, Acadia can in no sense be seen as a child of this great educational tradition. Certainly, Acadia was considerably influenced by the Scottish "common sense" philosophy, particularly as it came to Wolfville via American colleges,[54] but the college was never dominated by it. In this way, Acadia, more than many of her sister institutions at the time, was free to take what was useful from such a tradition without having the college pervaded by it. This freedom, potentially at least, made Acadia more open to new and conflicting ideas and philosophies and a place where serious intellectual inquiry *might*, in fact, take place.

It was then a fortuitous combination of a lack of an established denominational dogma, a diversity of background and philosophies, the concept of Christian education, concern for utilitarian training, a shortage of dominating personalities, and a variety of faculty members that produced the breadth and the flexibility that are such notable characteristics of Acadia College in the nineteenth century. And without the breadth and the flexibility, it is difficult to see how Acadia could have survived the early decades, let alone have finished the century as the largest college in the maritime provinces.

Building on such a foundation, Acadia College proved to be remarkably open to new ideas and directions. There seems to have been little in the field of education that its directors were not prepared at least to consider. Not, of course, that they adopted everything that came along, for financial, religious, or pedagogical considerations might militate against such acceptance. However, the college did prove very open to the winds of change that were blowing through the field of higher education in the nineteenth century. Perhaps nowhere is this more obvious than in the areas of female education and the struggle between science and religion.

When Horton Academy and Acadia College were founded, there was little serious consideration given to the education of females. The Baptists were concerned with establishing institutions to provide the necessary skills and the background for its young men to join the forward march of society. Women, it was supposed, would share indirectly in the general benefits that would thus result. In the maritime colonies, as elsewhere, there were very mixed feelings about providing a formal education for females.[55] However, there appear to have been no deeply entrenched, widely held views on the subject, thus opening the door to re-evaluation and change. Among maritime Baptists, those of New Brunswick took the lead in 1836 when they opened their new academy in Fredericton to male and female alike.[56] By the late 1840s, greatly influenced by developments in New England, maritime Baptists openly and extensively examined the issue of female education. In the long debate that ensued, the role played by men prominent in the affairs of Acadia was conspicuous. Differing views were expressed as to why females should be educated, and to what extent, but by the 1850s there appears to have been surprisingly little discussion over whether females should be educated. In the minds of many, the education of women became closely allied with, even a contributing factor to, all the other aspirations and designs of the Baptist body. As one anonymous writer to the *Christian Messenger* observed in 1849:

Unless something more is done properly to educate the female portion of the Baptist population, we shall scarcely hold our ground... Now until the mothers become better educated all hope of accomplishing our wishes will prove a failure... Woman's influence is powerful, much more so than we readily perceive; it is exerted so silently that we are not always aware of it. It is in proportion to the cultivation and refinement of nations, and is destined in my opinion to sway an untold power at no distant day in renovating this fallen world... and so we must believe that the education of females is not only in itself of overwhelming importance, but the *shortest cut* to the education of males.[57]

Several private schools for young ladies were opened by Baptists in the 1850s, while the next decade saw the beginnings of efforts by the denomination to provide education for their daughters as well as their sons at Wolfville.[58] Much of what they desired was summed up in one short phrase in a newspaper report: "Female Education, thorough, efficient and cheap."[59] Establishing a female seminary was one thing; admitting women to the full college course was obviously quite another. And yet for the Baptists of the maritime provinces it does not seem to have been a giant intellectual step. They had already challenged prevailing concepts of education for the lower classes; questioning restricted access to education on the basis of sex perhaps came relatively easily. By mid-century, few Baptists seemed willing openly to doubt the wisdom of providing as much education for a female as she was capable of handling. How this would be paid for, either by the individual family or by the denomination, and how such financial demands ranked in relation to the needs for male education seem to have been the overriding considerations, rather than the pedagogical or philosophical concerns that seemed to so preoccupy certain other North American bodies and institutions. As early as 1852, one writer to the *Christian Messenger*, after outlining what benefits to family, church, and society would be derived from female education, went on to state:

I must mention also the claims of females to a higher education, solely on *their own* account — the increase of happiness from more thought and knowledge, the highest sources of pleasure. Intellectual cultivation is indeed the *birth-right* of woman as a human being; and when this right is yielded, the effects are at once visible — in the greater activity and usefulness of females, in the increased happiness and altered tone of society, in the *intelligent* looks which meet the public speaker from his audiences, in the more refined atmosphere of domestic life; in the more rapid progress of mankind in all that is great and good.[60]

A few years later, one father writing to the press demolished the underpinnings of those opponents of higher education for females by holding their views up to ridicule. And in the process he asked that all-important question — why not? He argued, of course let the girls go to college as well.

Yes; educate the girls! Let them know how to knit and sew, how to make puddings, make the bread, the butter and the cheese; to sweep the floor, dust the chairs, darn the stockings, make the bed, and rock the cradle. But imagine not that these are the highest and holiest employments for which they are capable. Give them books. Put the pen into their hand. Let them look through the telescope into the heavens. Teach them botany, geology, chemistry, logic, language. Let them read Cicero, Virgil, Homer, Xenephon. Teach them Hebrew; teach them everything man needs to know.

[Let them attend the same classes with males?] Why not? — Do we live in Syria? in Turkey? in Hindostan? that our customs and laws require the entire separation of the sexes while they are growing up? [No!] We live in Nova Scotia, in North America, where time out of mind the boys and girls have been sent to school together, have sat upon the same benches, studied and read out of the same books, recited in the same class, and walked home in company. I never heard the practice denounced as either sin or shame ...

"Oh! but they would be thinking about one another, talking to one another, 'falling in love' with one another, writing love-letters, *courting*, and all that, as sure as rates, if they saw each other in School."

Would they indeed! What a phenomenon! Only think of it! boys and girls, young men and young women, actually thinking about each other! becoming fond of each other's company! and — mysterious! — amazing! — unheard-of event!! — actually thinking of matrimony!! and all this the result of sending them to learn Greek, Latin, French and Trigonometry together! ... Prevent the operation of Nature's laws, will you! Hinder the young people from *falling in love*. Ha! Not by sending them to different schools will you do it, I guess, and not by keeping them at home. When you can make a law and enforce it that the tide in the Bay of Fundy shall not ebb and flow: —

when you can command, as Joshua did, 'Sun, stand thou still upon Mt. Gideon! ... Then, not before, can you suppress these emotions, implanted in mortal bosoms by God himself, for the noblest and most benevolent of purposes. Out upon such nonsense![61]

It might be ridiculous nonsense to this sensible (one suspects, rural), writer and to many others in the colony at the time, but such ridiculed ideas would be taken very seriously indeed by many educators in North America and Europe for much of the rest of the century.[62]

Those who guided Acadia through these perilous waters seemed to share such common-sense views about higher education for females. Certainly Crawley and Sawyer, at least, among the presidents were in favour of opening wide the doors of the college. As early as 1874 President Sawyer had recommended such a step to the Board of Governors.[63] Financial considerations would delay the beginning of female education at Acadia until 1880, but when it came it caused scarcely a ripple. It did not even require a special resolution of the Board of Governors; it was merely done. The following year the board informed the Convention of the action taken, observing that "Thus the privileges of the college will henceforth be open to the sons and daughters of the land, and on the same conditions."[64] (It should be noted that it was obviously not considered necessary to seek the Convention's approval even for such a major departure from past practice.) A year later the board's report to Convention laconically remarked: "As yet there are no indications that a mistake was made in admitting young women to the privileges of the College."[65] In 1884 Acadia awarded its first degree to a female graduate, the second institution in the British Empire to take such a step.

The willingness of Acadia College, and many maritime Baptists, to extend their vision of education to include the female portion of the population is, it may be argued, further evidence of a broadly based, flexible approach to education, one that had not yet hardened into rigidity. Such could not be said of every college in Canada in the nineteenth century.

Another example, among many, of the way in which such flexibility shaped the contours of the college and greatly strengthened what the institution stood for may be seen in Acadia's response to the growing tension between science and religion in the latter half of the nineteenth century. The scientific discoveries of the age and the theories that they spawned had much of the Christian Church in turmoil. The age of Darwin had dawned. If the churches of Christendom had difficulty dealing with the issues raised, so did the colleges. How could one pursue knowledge and truth in the laboratory and the classroom if it led one to question the divinely revealed truths found in the scriptures? Yet not to pursue knowledge as far as one could go seemed to be the abandonment of all that a college had traditionally stood for. But would not, and did not, rational inquiry lead to skepticism?[66]

Many North American and British academics and theologians strove to grapple with these perplexing problems in the years following the publication of Darwin's *The Origin of Species* in 1859. The academics and theologians at Acadia College were no exception. One might have expected to find among maritime Baptists outright condemnation and then dismissal of Darwin and of the new scientific knowledge and theories. Instead, one finds a calm, temperate debate, from which hysterical over reaction seems largely absent. Those maritime Baptists who wrote and spoke in the debate between science and religion expressed as one would expect a variety of views. As with so many other issues during this period of time, there seems to have been no orthodox Baptist position to defend, no generally agreed upon stand to take. The response, then, was not to recoil in horror but to examine and debate, in a way not always possible, perhaps, in some other denominations and institutions in Canada.

Throughout the 1850s and 60s at Acadia, scientific exploration was often lauded as part of the means by which mankind would advance. The enthusiasm for science of Isaac Chipman, and his stature within the denomination and the college, certainly made science a respected, even essential, part of the college curriculum. Many welcomed the new methods since, as one writer observed in 1867: "Induction and demonstration have taken the place of conjecture and hypothesis." He remarked further:

United with the most powerful energies of Christianity, science has raised the human mind from a fearful depth of degradation; and we foresee that day as near, when by their co-operation, united with Art, the intellectual and moral powers of man shall be mightily enlarged and purified.[67]

J.M. Cramp, while primarily a theologian and church historian, was fascinated with scientific discovery and speculation. For example, in the mid-1850s he gave a talk both in Halifax and in Wolfville that explored the possibility of human life on other planets. Although he concluded that it was impossible to ascertain for certain, he argued that it was highly likely that such life did exist. Such a view, with its obvious theological implications, elicited no anguished cry of outrage. In fact, there is no evidence of any response at all.[68] Science fascinated, perplexed and mystified, but it does not seem to have frightened.

The upheaval following the publication of Darwin's ideas does not seem to have shaken Cramp's faith in the importance of scientific exploration and discovery. As he told Acadia's graduating class of 1867,

Apart from the gratification which such studies afford, and their bearing on intellectual progress, the connection of science with religion is so intimate and important that every true friend of the one should seek to be well acquainted with the other. So far from being antagonistic, as is frequently affirmed, they contribute mutual illustration and help. Nothing less could be expected. The works and the word of God must be in full harmony ... God cannot contradict in one book what he has written in another ... Reason and faith are twin sisters. Faith is vindicated by reason, and reason is dignified by faith. The discoveries and researches of modern times have shed a flood of light on the divine record, and removed numerous obscurities which have long seemed impenetrable. We rejoice in the labours of the genuine philosopher, and welcome him as an ally in the warfare with evil. Let us be willing, too, to receive his instructions and follow him when he leads us into the 'deep things of God' — the wonders and intricacies of material laws. We have no reason to fear the results; and at any rate, if we admit scientific enlightenment, we shall not be deceived by plausible but crude theories or carried away by hasty generalizations. But there may be much danger if we are willingly ignorant of these matters, since we may become an easy prey to cunning and malicious unbelievers.[69]

Darwinian views created discord and consternation in many places in the western world. However, at a surprisingly early stage, the reconciliation of science and religion had already begun at Acadia

College under a faculty and a denomination that was still broadly enough based to absorb even the shocks of Darwinism. And, moreover, they were able to see something very positive in the whole confrontation.[70]

That such views were not merely the private musings of a few Baptist intellectuals and faculty members is made very clear when one examines some of the student essays and orations of the period. In his graduating essay in 1870, one student, perhaps slightly carried away by his topic, argued that everywhere

Positivism and New Testament Christianity confront each other ... The philosopher dishonours his badge when he sneers at religion; and the theologian belittles himself and his profession when he ignores discovery through fear, or protests against logic and inquiry as though they must needs be godless. The day of accord must come. Faith whose intolerance may have impelled science to go off like a prodigal will yearn after the wanderer, and go out to meet him while yet afar off; and science sick of rioting and husks will turn homeward penitent and wiser ... Prayer and study will stimulate each other. Philosophy will be devout, and religion will be discriminating... The lecturer and the preacher will have a common aim, the Darwins and the Spurgeons mutually give and take; and a rounded manhood will appear as the fruit of a civilization which has taken up all wholesome elements to feed its vigorous body.[71]

Even the spirited defence in 1870 of T.H. Huxley by the Acadia science professor, William Elder, could not arouse much debate within the Baptist community. While acknowledging that Huxley was one of the leading advocates of the theory of evolution, Elder saw no reason to condemn him out of hand, arguing that

Notwithstanding these dangerous looking words, I think it would be only fair to read his own expressions of his views, and find out whether they really do clash with Revelation before we condemn them.

Whether or not the blood corpuscles are identical with the ultimate materials of other substances, animal and vegetable, is a question to be decided by scientific investigation not by pathetic prose or interjectional bathos. A belief in the affirmative does not seem to me to threaten the safety of the Church.[72]

Such a statement brought only one letter of criticism, and then one letter of support. There was no censure by the Board of Governors; in fact the incident is not mentioned in the board minutes. Nor is there any indication that the matter was even raised in a single Baptist church in the maritimes.

Acadia was able to cope intellectually with the trauma of the new age partially at least because of its perception of Christian education and the broad base upon which the institution so firmly stood. It had been able to accommodate so many ideas, to incorporate such a wide diversity of opinion, that it was probably better prepared than many such colleges to withstand the challenge of these new concepts. An earlier writer had admonished his readers to "Go first to God and then to College," and all other things would fall into their proper places.[73] President Sawyer argued much the same thing in his report to Convention in 1874. All will be well if we "make religion the foundation of the structure and all branches of human knowledge the materials ... science and religion should not be considered as antagonistic forces, but rather as different methods of reading and understanding the purposes of God."[74]

In their approach to the challenges of science, the issue of higher education for females, in new programs for the college and the community, and in so many other ways, Acadia and the Baptists revealed a breadth of vision and a breadth of mind remarkably free of fear or narrow prejudice, sectarian or otherwise. This is not to suggest that nineteenth-century Baptists did not have their blind spots, where vision was clouded by intolerance and the direction uncertain. What one does see is a quite astonishing willingness to at least consider the various alternatives, to explore where perhaps some others were afraid to do so. Having developed as a denomination by challenging some of the orthodoxies of both church and state, and having as yet no collective orthodoxy of their own to defend, they were free to revel in the new intellectual realms that had opened up for them with the establishment of Acadia College. It would have its pitfalls as well as its benefits, of course, but while it lasted such an open approach brought with it a strength and a vitality that were notable features of the college in the last century.

Interestingly enough, such developments within the dissenting tradition have been largely ignored by those historians who would attempt to understand the intellectual origins of twentieth-century

Canada. Focusing largely on Anglican and Presbyterian thinkers and writers (usually British born and resident in Upper Canada), with a token Methodist or two, gives only part of the picture, one overly dominated by the long shadow of Great Britain. Until the dissenting contribution to the intellectual development of Canada is taken more seriously, partial understandings, half truths, and distorted images are likely to result. The contribution of the Baptists in general, and of Acadia College in particular, has been seriously undervalued, by intellectual historians but also by Baptists as well. The long-supposed unintellectual, even anti-intellectual, Baptists of the nineteenth-century maritimes may yet be shown to have contributed something of considerable significance to the intellectual development of Canada.

In an address to the students at Acadia at the commencement of term, September 1870, Edmund Crawley attempted to articulate his concerns in a talk entitled "Freedom of Thought." According to the press report, he condemned "alike the boasted liberality which runs to license and the intolerance that cannot brook inquiry. He pointed out the necessity of opposing all errors, scientific and religious in the most open manner by the most fair and honest means. His noble plea for that intellectual independence which we as Baptists are especially bound to contend for cannot fail to be beneficial to those who heard it."[75] Clearly a long, careful look at the nineteenth-century intellectual development of Acadia College and of the maritime Baptists is called for; the surface has only been scratched. And when we have examined fully that "intellectual independence which we as Baptists are especially bound to contend for," perhaps then will become apparent the full significance of what the founders and guardians of Acadia College actually accomplished.

A.L. McCrimmon,
H.P. Whidden, T.T. Shields,
Christian Education,
and McMaster University

The granting of McMaster University's charter in 1887 was both a new beginning and a culmination "of Baptist educational ventures that reached far back into pre-Confederation Canada."[1] The McMaster of 1887, in other words, was as Professor Charles Johnston has persuasively argued, made up of historical segments from the Canada Baptist College in Montreal, the Canadian Literary Institute in Woodstock, and the Toronto Baptist College and Moulton College of Toronto. But, of course, McMaster University was also much more than this. It was also the creation of Senator William McMaster, a native of Tyrone County, Ireland, who had by the 1870s become one of Canada's most influential entrepreneurs and also a leading Reform politician. A staunch advocate of the commercial imperialism of Toronto, McMaster used his presidency of the Bank of Commerce to "establish a commercial dominion at least the equal of Montreal's."[2] His ardent support of the Reform cause of George Brown and Alexander MacKenzie, led to McMaster's appointment to the Canadian Senate in 1867.

McMaster was more than an unusually successful Canadian entrepreneur and politician. He was also a pious and committed evangelical Baptist who was particularly concerned with doing everything humanly possible to improve the educational standards of his denomination's ministers as well as its laypeople. Like many other leading Canadian Baptists in the latter part of the nineteenth century, McMaster was obsessed with the desperate search for denominational respectability. One important way to achieve this end, it was felt, was to build a respectable Baptist university. Another

way was to construct a Baptist cathedral — the new Jarvis Street
Baptist Church — which took ostentatious new Gothic shape in
Toronto in 1876 under the direction of Senator and Mrs. McMaster.
According to William Davies, the founder of a famous Canadian
packing firm and a bitter critic of the McMasters:

this large Baptist Chapel, gothic, brown stone, spire pointing upward if not
heavenward, marble baptistry etc. etc. Cost $100,000 and odd and the organ
$7000 besides, and I believe it is all paid for, but it has been built regardless
of the needs of the city … One of the members … a Senator, very wealthy,
married an American, natural result they soon had an American minister,
then this new building also American, then the Lady and the minister lay
their heads together and get a professional singer a sort of *prima donna* and
she is paid $300.00 per year and many are very much hurt about it … There
appears to have been a spirit of centralization and aggrandizement about it
which is hateful.[3]

Davies' caustic comments contain a ring of truth. The McMasters
were indeed interested in "centralization and aggrandizement" and
in the early 1880s they tended to think that what was good for them
was excellent for their less fortunate coreligionists.

By 1879 the McMasters and some of their Toronto Baptist friends
had come to the conclusion that a Baptist institution of higher learning had to be built in the capital of Ontario. The Canadian Literary
Institute in Woodstock, they had to admit, was more than adequate
in terms of its elementary and secondary programs. However, they
were just as convinced that the institute's theological department
had to be transferred to Toronto, since a respectable and progressive
Baptist university had no real future in Woodstock. At the 1879 Baptist Convention at Guelph, it was decided, after a very heated
debate, and with at least an implicit understanding that McMaster
money would pay for the new Toronto institution and also significantly subsidize the ongoing Baptist educational effort in Woodstock, that a new "theological seminary" be established.

According to the 1 December 1880 Act incorporating the Toronto
Baptist College, the college was under the control of a Board of Trustees carefully selected by Senator McMaster and his American-born
pastor, the Reverend John Castle. According to the deed of trust, the
trustees were

to permit the use and occupation of said buildings ... for the necessary and proper purposes of a theological college ... for the education and training of students preparing for and intending to be engaged in pastoral, evangelical, missionary or other denominational work in connection with the Regular Baptist Denomination whereby is intended Regular Baptist Churches exclusively composed of persons who have been baptized on a personal profession of their Faith in Christ holding and maintaining *substantially* the following doctrines.[4]

It is important to note that the deed of trust does explicitly state, before listing its strong calvinist evangelical statement of faith, that those Baptists associated with the new "theological college" had only to hold and maintain "*substantially* the following doctrines." For some Baptists, even in 1880, "*substantially*" was not any kind of qualifier but rather the emphatic underscoring of orthodoxy.

The "following doctrines" were:

The Divine Inspiration of the Scriptures of the Old and New Testaments and their absolute Supremacy and Sufficiency in matters of faith and practice; the existence of one living and true God, sustaining the personal relation of Father Son and Holy Spirit, the same in essence and equal in attributes, the total and universal depravity of mankind, the election and effectual calling of all God's people, the atoning efficacy of the Death of Christ, the free justification of believers in Him by His imputed Righteousness; the preservation unto eternal life of the Saints, the necessity and efficacy of the influence of the Spirit in regeneration and sanctification; the resurrection of the dead, both just and unjust; the general judgment, the everlasting happiness of the righteous and the everlasting misery of the wicked; immersion in the name of the Father the Son and the Holy Spirit, the only gospel "baptism," that parties so baptized are alone entitled to Communion at the Lord's Table and that a Gospel Church is a Body of baptized believers voluntarily associated together for the service of God.[5]

What did the deed of trust, which was an integral part of the Toronto Baptist College Act of Incorporation, actually mean? Did it mean that everyone teaching or being taught in the college had to hold "substantially" to such a statement of faith? No, the widely accepted legal interpretation was quite different. As far as one noted legal expert — N.W. Rowell — was concerned the "theological tests or requirements set out in the Trust Deed" were not "tests or require-ments" applied to the institution but were "tests or requirements applied to the Baptist Denomination entitled to control the University and have its theological students taught" there. Therefore, and this point needs to be stressed, because of its important implications for McMaster University in the 1920s, "the only way in which" McMaster's institution "could be affected" by anyone "challenging its theological teaching would be by their challenging the theological standing of the Baptist Denomination represented and in forming the Baptist Convention of Ontario and Quebec."[6]

McMaster carefully selected the trustees for the Toronto Baptist College and these men, on the whole, reflected the senator's commercial and political views. There were leading lawyers, businessmen, and politicians such as Alexander MacKenzie, the former Liberal prime minister of Canada. What these men seemed to have in common was a tremendous commitment to the Baptist cause in Ontario and Quebec as well as a profound belief in the efficacy of higher education. Moreover, led and inspired by McMaster, they were preoccupied with the quest for power and influence, not only in Canadian society but also within their own denomination.

By controlling the Baptist seminary in central Canada, which they hoped would quickly "emerge as a national institution for the denomination,"[7] they expected to control the entire denomination from the top down. According to Antonio Gramsci, cultural hegemony in a society being transformed by industrial capitalism is characterized by "the spontaneous consent given by the great masses of the population to the general direction imposed on social life by the dominant fundamental group; this consent is 'historically' caused by prestige (and consequent confidence) which the dominant group enjoys because of its position and function in the world of production."[8] For Gramsci, organized religion plays a crucially important role in the actual exercise of power of one group over another. It should not be forgotten that, as Tom Harpur has recently pointed out, "from one very important point of view, the whole of organized religion is a not-too-subtle form of power-seeking and control."[9] Christian feminists for years have been making this precise point about misogyny and the power structure of the Christian Church. Their analysis and that of Gramsci and his disciples, in my view, can be powerfully applied to the development in the nineteenth and twentieth centuries of the Christian Church in North America in general and to the Baptist denomination in Canada in particular.

It is Gramsci's contention that the new class of capitalistic entre-preneurs — the McMasters of this world — concern themselves with the creation of a new "strata of intellectuals" whose role it is "to win over the traditional strata to support... the new social, economic, and political order." For Gramsci, in new societies like that of Canada in the 1880s, the new group of intellectuals are expected to "fuse together in a single national crucible with a unitary culture the diffe-rent forms of culture imported by immigrants of differing national origins."[10] This fusing process facilitates economic growth in a coun-try like Canada and helps to explain why all Protestant churches in Canada in the pre-1914 period were so preoccupied with building an anglophile and Christian "Dominion from sea to sea."[11]

It was also Gramsci's contention that the new class of intellectuals, including, of course, the religious leaders, are locked into an integra-tive symbiotic relationship with a new social order thrown up by the fundamental changes affecting economic production. The intellec-tual-priest thus functions at two levels, which "correspond on the one hand to the function of 'hegemony' which the dominant group exercises throughout society and on the other hand to that of 'direct domination' — a command exercised through the state ... The func-tions in question are precisely organizational and connective. The intellectuals are the dominant group's 'deputies' exercising the sub-altern functions of social hegemony and political government."[12]

Thus, if we use a Gramsci-like lens to view unfolding events in the Toronto and Ontario Baptist community in the 1880s, a disconcerting picture suddenly emerges — McMaster and his Baptist business asso-ciates may be seen as calculating entrepreneurs determined to create their own battalion of ministerial "deputies," expertly trained to impose suitable hegemonic order and control over Canadian society.

Even though McMaster and his associates considered themselves to be staunch protectors of the pristine purity of evangelical calvinist Baptist orthodoxy, they were also committed advocates of the new North American consumer culture. And because of this, they offered what has been called "a new legitimization"[13] for the antithesis of calvinist evangelical orthodoxy — a narcissistic gospel of intense "therapeutic self-realization." In the 1880s and 1890s in North

America "the leaders of the W.A.S.P. bourgeoisie," it has been observed, "felt cramped," over-civilized, "cut off from real life — threatened from without by an ungrateful working class, and from within by their own sense of physical atrophy and spiritual decay." Moreover,

The old religious sanctions for the moral life, a life of sacrifice and toil, had begun to disintegrate in the face of both Darwin and the liberalization of Protestantism itself. A crisis of purpose, a yearning for a solid, transcendent framework of meaning, was not just Henry Adams' worry, but that of a much wider group. In this time of cultural consternation, the new professional-managerial corps appeared with a timely dual message. On the one hand, they preached a new morality that subordinated the old goal of transcendence to new ideals of self-fulfillment and immediate gratification. The late nineteenth-century link between individual hedonism and bureaucratic organization — a link that has been strengthened in the twentieth century — marks the point of departure for modern American consumer culture. The consumer culture is not only the value-system that underlies a society saturated by mass-produced and mass-marketed goods, but also a new set of sanctions for the elite control of that society.[14]

This inner transformation of North American society is of critical importance to any sophisticated understanding of late nineteenth- and early twentieth-century historical and theological development. The prevailing Whig scholarly concern with progress and modernity has meant, among other things, however, that most historians simply assume that by the turn of the century the North American evangelical consensus was being shattered by three powerful external forces. First, there was Darwin and evolution and the new science; then there was critical biblical scholarship; and third there was the impact of comparative religion which seemed to undermine, for many, the belief in the uniqueness of Christianity. Without question, these three forces certainly helped to reshape the contours of North American Protestantism.[15] Yet it may also be argued that in the long run American consumerism may have had a far greater negative impact on the nineteenth-century evangelical consensus than did the various manifestations of so-called modern scholarship. In other words, a convincing case may be put forward that the evangelical consensus suffered more from internal decay than from external attacks. And at the core of this decay, as D.W. Frank has recently contended, was the cancer of consumerism — "based on self-indulgence."[16] The testimony of a woman visiting some eighty years ago a department store, the key economic institution of the consumer society, cuts to the heart of the issue:

I felt myself overcome little by little by a disorder that can only be compared to that of drunkenness, with the dizziness and excitation that are peculiar to it. I saw things as if through a cloud, everything stimulated my desire and assumed, for me, an extraordinary attraction. I felt myself swept along toward them and I grabbed hold of things without any outside and superior consideration intervening to hold me back. Moreover I took things at random, useless and worthless articles as well as useful and expensive articles. It was like a monomania of possession.[17]

Other women made similar comments — "my head was spinning," "I felt completely dizzy," "I am just as if I were drunk." These comments were made by middle class women who had been arrested for shoplifting. They were, it has been observed, "an odd foreshadowing of Billy Sunday's contention that alcohol was the cause of virtually all crime." The women's addiction, however, was "to consumer gratification." "The pathological frenzy to which some women were driven," it is clear, "had become simply the seamier side of the new consumer society, where the old virtues of thrift and self-control were giving way to a culture of gratification."[18] These women, drunk on goods, were striking symbols of the new consumer society.

It seemed impossible for evangelical leaders — whether in Canada or in the United States — in the post-1880 period to attack frontally the insidious anti-Christian bias of consumerism. Instead, they became, the evidence seems to suggest, its ardent disciples and enthusiastic advocates of the fundamental goodness of economic growth and technological development. They were certainly unwilling to see what Karl Marx saw in "modern bourgeois society" in the 1880s and beyond. For Marx, such a society "has conjured up such gigantic means of production and of exchange" and has in the process become "like the sorcerer who is no longer able to control the powers of the subterranean which he has called up by his spells." Marx then went on: "Constant revolutionizing of production, uninterrupted disturbance of all social relations, everlasting uncertainty and agitation, distinguish the bourgeois epoch from all earlier ones. All fixed, fast-frozen relations, with their train of ancient and venerable prejudices and opinions, are swept away, all new-formed ones become antiquated before they can ossify. All that is solid melts into air, all that is holy is profane."[19] Marx had laid bare the essential nature of life in modernizing society and he had realized intuitively what had happened to North American evangelicalism. The "holy" had, in a profound sense, become "profane" and "all that" was "solid" had melted into nothingness.

Few, if any, central Canadian Baptists in the 1880s would have, or more accurately, could have, accepted the validity of Marx's penetrating prophetic insight into the essential nature of bourgeois-industrial society. And this was certainly the case with regard to McMaster and his Baptist business associates. Yet, as the nineteenth century blurred into the twentieth, and after McMaster's death in 1887, a few Baptists came to realize that something fundamentally destructive was beginning to undermine the theological and ideological underpinnings of their church and their society. But instead of focusing, as Marx had done, on the distinguishing features of the "bourgeois society" or, as others had done, on the evils of "consumerism," these disconcerted Baptists concentrated their concern on what to them was theological modernism — the way in which Darwinian scientific progress and biblical scholarship were significantly altering the older evangelical consensus. These Baptists and their supporters in other Protestant denominations would soon become known as fundamentalists and their growing obsession with preserving theological purity would be matched by a remarkable degree of "violence in thought and language."[20] These people would find it far easier to be judgmental than forgiving, destructive rather than constructive, and confrontational rather than accommodating. But these people, it should be stressed, were not the mainstream of evangelicalism at the turn of the century. They found themselves on one extreme of a broad theological spectrum which stretched all the way to the closed-minded liberalism of some who, in attempting to make Christianity especially relevant to the new age, made it virtually as irrelevant as themselves. At the centre of the Baptist theological spectrum was to be found the evangelical mainstream — the vast majority of Baptists

— who accepted basic evangelical truths and who were not really afraid of modernity. These people *felt* their religion — in other words, they experienced it — and they therefore saw no compelling need to intellectualize it. They expected their ministers to preach the old-time gospel but also to make it relevant to their situation.

Between the evangelical mainstream and the liberal extreme was to be found a very influential group that was eager to keep a foot in both camps. Its approach was permeated by an accommodationist spirit — what has been recently referred to as "a new hermeneutic" based on a "double commitment: to the biblical faith on the one hand and the modern outlook on the other."[21] Such individuals became the "intellectual-priests" of the emerging central Canadian Baptist commercial elite. In the 1880–1914 period, however, these men were not yet in complete control and found themselves challenged by yet another group — not as accommodating to modernity and somewhat more sympathetic to the theological underpinnings of fundamentalism — although certainly not to its increasing *hubris* and paranoia. Such individuals, some of whom were academics, were, like their fundamentalist friends, also fully aware of the contagion of change which was reshaping the boundaries of their society. Their answer to the problem was the careful constructing of intellectual barriers to protect the purity of the faith — but these barriers were put up in such a manner as to permit and to encourage the flow of new ideas. The barriers of the fundamentalists, however, left no space for these ideas. And the liberals, of course — their intense intellectual arrogance notwithstanding — prided themselves on having no barriers whatsoever.

The fundamentalists, the so-called liberal evangelicals, the conservative evangelicals, and the liberals were all concerned about higher education. And within the central Canadian Baptist community in the late nineteenth and early twentieth centuries the academic battle involved, in the beginning, the first three groups. But with the polarization of the theological debate in the years surrounding the First World War, the educational controversy began to involve only two sets of antagonists — the liberal evangelicals (who were becoming almost more liberal than evangelical) and the fundamentalists — some of whom were former advocates of a more moderate conservative evangelical position. This ideological split, it should be stressed, was buttressed by growing class tensions between the two groups, what Dr. Walter Ellis has described as "class war in the churches."[22] Bourgeois liberal respectability was warring against what one Baptist liberal evangelical referred to as fundamentalist "bigotry, and fanaticism and obscurantism."[23] The perceived class differences existing between the two groups were superbly captured in a letter written to S.J. Moore, a Toronto Baptist millionaire in November 1926, by a shrewd observer of the fundamentalist-modernist split in the Convention: "I was impressed by the personnel of the majority. It included ... nearly all the solid elements of the denomination. As the followers of Dr. Shields gathered about him at the close of the meeting, to join in their singing and other emotional manifestations, I could not but be impressed by the inferior personnel of the group. I am speaking of the general appearance."[24] It was a simple Manichean struggle between the "solid elements" and the "inferior personnel," between progress and backwardness, between the past and the future.

It is against this richly complex ideological and cultural backdrop that one must view evolving central Canadian Baptist attitudes towards Christian higher education at the turn of the century. To see the problem within strictly institutional or denominational parameters is to distort significantly historical reality and also to avoid some disconcerting problems relating to essential motivation. The Baptist educational experience, moreover, was not static but rather dynamic and constantly changing, influenced by people, events, and ideas, but always evolving within the context of what some might regard as Gramsci reality.

Senator McMaster and his Baptist friends were not satisfied for long merely with a "theological institute." During the early 1880s, they applied considerable pressure on their coreligionists and finally, on 15 March 1887, a bill was introduced at Queen's Park uniting the Toronto Baptist College and Woodstock College and incorporating them as McMaster University. On 22 April 1887, the Act of Incorporation became law; and exactly five months later Senator McMaster died, leaving close to $1,000,000 to his university. "The monumental irony of the situation," McMaster University's historian has noted, "struck even the most insensitive." "At one stroke the university that McMaster had promoted was instantly financed but at the cost of his vigour, direction, and inspiration."[25]

Section four of McMaster University's Act of Incorporation made it clear that the university was definitely "a Christian school of learning." It went on:

the study of the Bible, or sacred scriptures, shall form a part of the course of study taught by the professors, tutors, or masters appointed by the Board of Governors. And no person shall be eligible to the position of chancellor, principal, professor, tutor, or master, who is not a member in good standing of an Evangelical Christian Church; and no person shall be eligible for the position of principal, professor, tutor, or master in the faculty of theology who is not a member in good standing of a Regular Baptist Church, and the said Board of Governors shall have the right to require such further or other tests as to religious belief, as a qualification for any position in the faculty of theology, as to the said Board of Governors may seem proper; but no compulsory religious qualification, or examination of a denominational character shall be required from, or imposed upon any student whatever, other than in the faculty of theology.[26]

It is evident from the 1887 Act of Incorporation that, while McMaster University was to be a Christian institution, only its seminary was to be explicitly Baptist. There was to be no theological litmus test for McMaster students but all university teachers and officials were to be "Evangelical Christians" — and the faculty of theology were to be evangelical Baptists, broadly defined, who could be subjected by the Board of Governors to some kind of "test as to religious belief." Taking everything into account, the act, in many respects, was quite progressive in tone and content but so much, of course, depended on what was meant by the phrase "Christian school of learning" and "Evangelical Christian Church." The underlying assumption of the act, however, was crystal clear. Students at McMaster would be educated by evangelical Christian teachers in a Christian environment so that they would "be thoroughly equipped with all the resources of the best and most liberal culture to enable them to meet the polished shafts of a refined and subtle infidelity."[27]

The third chancellor of McMaster University, the Reverend OCS Wallace, enunciated in his inaugural address in 1895 what he must have realized was a strong defence for Christian higher education. He was widely regarded as a staunch defender of the evangelical *status quo* but he was also known as someone very concerned about preparing his "students for the challenges of life in the outer world."[28] Though a pious traditionalist in one sense, Wallace was also, as his later career would show, determined to make Christianity relevant for modern society. He was not opposed, therefore, to a shift in Protestant theology from a preoccupation with "salvation in the next world to therapeutic self-realization in this one."[29]

As far as Wallace was concerned, in 1895 McMaster University existed "for the teaching rather than the pursuit of truth." "Much of the educational work of the present day," he went on

is a menace to all that is holiest in faith and loftiest in morality because it is moulded in form and determined in spirit by the contrary of that principle ... We are not denying that there is truth to pursue, but we do most confidently and solemnly affirm that there is truth to teach. However vast may be the domain of the unexplored and the unknown, it is yet true that something is known [and is] ours by the ... attestation of the ages [or] by the unequivocal revelation of God ... Before such truths as have been abundantly proven or clearly revealed we dare not take the attitude of the ... doubter and the agnostic ... It is our aim to send forth ... scholars whose opinions of truth and whose principles of conduct shall not be ... a source and occasion of irreligion in the communities in which they live.[30]

Some of Wallace's friends, however, did not accept the new chancellor's point of view. One of them informed him:

When once that spirit — that 'a university exists for the teaching rather than the pursuit of truth' — has laid hold of an institution its zenith has been reached. Like the perfectionists in character no advance is believed possible, no advance will be made ... every truth that is not brought home to the individual conscience and judgment and there accepted as truth on its own merits is, to a student, a worse than useless incumbrance ... I believe in the scientific method, the method that is used in all good schools at the present day ... and which the sentence quoted opposes. There is a wide difference between the scientific search for truth and the agnostic search for ignorance.[31]

By the time of his resignation in 1905, Wallace had moved quite a distance in the direction of his friend's position of encouraging "the scientific search for truth" in order to make McMaster into a "good," modern university.[32] In his journey, the Nova Scotia born educator was encouraged by some of his board members, as well as some of his faculty — especially those who were scientists. Yet Wallace would never abandon his commitment to the "development of a generous and noble" Christian character.[33]

Wallace's successor as chancellor was A.C. McKay, who for years had been the key administrative factotum at McMaster. He played a key role in keeping McMaster a separate educational institution by leading the fight against federation with the University of Toronto. McKay was enthusiastically committed to "the scientific search for truth" and he seemed to be amazingly indifferent to the growing theological civil war between so-called liberals and fundamentalists being fought in the Convention and in his theology faculty. What came to be known as the "Matthews Controversy" reached a crisis point in 1908 and 1909. The critics of Professor I.G. Matthews — the Chicago trained Old Testament scholar — argued that Matthews was a pernicious modernist determined to destroy the orthodox faith of his theological students. To counter the growing fundamentalist movement in the Convention, McKay saw the need for McMaster's Senate to emphasize the institution's theological orthodoxy — but without abandoning his belief in the efficacy of science and modern scholarship. An investigating committee submitted its report to the Senate on 29 May 1909 and it declared Matthews innocent of the charges of unorthodoxy. Though he accepted many of the "results of critical scholarship" he nevertheless "held firmly to the inspiration and supernatural character of the Old and New Testaments." Then the Senate boldly declared:

McMaster stands for freedom, for progress, for investigation. It must welcome truth from whatever quarter, and never be guilty of binding the spirit of free enquiry. As a Christian school of learning under Baptist auspices, it stands for the fullest and freest investigation, not only in the scientific realm but also in the realm of Biblical scholarship. Holding fast their historic position on the personal freedom and responsibility of the individual, refusing to bind or be bound by any human creed, rejecting the authority of tradition and taking their stand on the word of God alone as the supreme and all-sufficient rule of faith and practice, the Baptists have ever been ready to accord to all students of the Sacred Scriptures the largest possible measure of freedom consistent with loyalty to the fundamentals of the Christian faith.[34]

At the 2 December 1909 Senate meeting, it was agreed that "while complete freedom should be accorded in the investigation and discussion of facts no theory should be taught in [the] University which fails to give their proper place to supernatural revelation ... or which would impair in any way the supreme authority of the Lord Jesus Christ."[35]

When the "Matthews Controversy" was brought to the floor of the Convention in October 1910, the Senate position was endorsed by a large majority. A leader in this movement to prevent a Convention denunciation of McMaster and Matthews was the Reverend T.T. Shields, the minister of Jarvis Street Baptist Church and a leading fundamentalist in the Convention. Shields probably did not want to alienate in 1910 some of his key church members who were keen supporters of Matthews and McKay.

The Senate response to the "Matthews Controversy" is important in at least two ways with respect to Baptists and Christian higher education in central Canada. First, McMaster's Senate and also the Convention explicitly endorsed the key role of higher education in bringing about human "progress" — bourgeois progress and consumerism. Second, it was emphatically agreed that accommodation was indeed possible between the evangelical consensus and the new scholarship. And, moreover, it was contended that McMaster University had a special role in bringing about this accommodation which, for some, was merely the articulation of the liberal evangelical point of view.

By 1911, McKay had come to the realization that he was "not born to be in the midst of theological controversy."[36] He therefore resigned as chancellor to become principal of a new technical high school in Toronto. Many Baptists were genuinely sorry to see McKay leave McMaster. Others were not, feeling that he was too soft on modernism and liberalism. They looked for someone a little more spiritual, a little more pious, a little more evangelical, to replace him. They saw such a person in Abraham Lincoln McCrimmon.

McCrimmon was born in 1865 on a farm a mile north of Delhi in western Ontario. He graduated from the University of Toronto in 1890 as gold medalist in logic and philosophy. As a student at the University of Toronto, he excelled not only in his studies but also in athletics. A fine pitcher, he once "struck out twelve men consecutively" and it was said "that he was one of the first exponents in

Ontario of the curve ball."[37] When he graduated, therefore, McCrimmon had to choose between Christian service and a career in professional baseball. He gladly chose the former. In 1892, he became classics master at Woodstock College and five years later, he became its principal. While at Woodstock, McCrimmon showed that he "possessed one of the finest intellects among the educational leaders of America."[38] As a preacher and platform speaker, the former baseball star began to "rank with the most polished and forceful orators in the country."[39] He was widely perceived as an "intensely religious and ever zealous" Baptist, who always "sought to convey the message of God in clear and convincing language."[40] Until his death in 1935, McCrimmon regarded himself as an unreconstructed Baptist evangelical; an advocate of "soul-liberty," he always "made the necessity of regeneration ... the centre of my message to a lost world."[41] Moreover, throughout his teaching career, he regarded, as he once put it, "My relationship to my students" as a "sacred relationship." It was based upon mutual confidence and respect and "spiritual power."[42]

During the 1903–4 academic year, McCrimmon pursued graduate studies at the University of Chicago. And on his return to Woodstock, he was appointed, while still principal of Woodstock College, to a lectureship in political economy at McMaster University. In 1906, he was persuaded to leave Woodstock and join the faculty of McMaster as a "full time Professor, occupying the Chair of Economics, Education and Sociology."[43]

In 1893, the year after he began teaching at Woodstock College, McCrimmon published a very brief description of his philosophy of Christian education. As far as the twenty-eight-year-old McCrimmon was concerned, "the Highest Type of Human Character is Therefore the Christian Character. The Ideal For the Christian [and for Christian Education] is Jesus Christ, As Revealed in the Word of God ... Here we have combined the absolute surrender of individuality and its most intense assertion."[44] Eight years later, McCrimmon developed his educational ideas at much greater length when he spoke at Brandon College, on 1 October 1901, on the topic "Christian Education."[45] According to McCrimmon, "While it is the inalienable right of every man to have an education, it is the doubly emphasized responsibility for the Christian whose heart should be tender to God's teaching and whose will should be ready and anxious to do his work." Moreover, only Christian education moulded the youthful mind in the image of Christ. The Woodstock principal then went on to assert that at the core of Christian education was the person of Christ:

Our starting point is that we hold our connection with Christ as the supreme element in our lives. Identification with Him brings salvation to our souls. Identification with Him means that His thoughts are our thoughts and His work is our work. If we rear a structure whether of personal attainment or of objective work, which has not the purpose of Christ in it, it means that the work perishes. Not every education will do. We desire not knowledge alone but that knowledge rightly articulated to the work of Christ.

For McCrimmon, true "Christian Education" had to — as he expressed it — "Honour the Body" and "the Intellect." Christian education was not only concerned with shaping the minds of students but also with "the condition of the body." McCrimmon's Christian school was definitely not "some sort of goody-goody establishment where intellectual powers are at a discount." Rather, "The greatest intellects of this world are the intellects of Christian men ... It is only the Christian who has the proper motive to instigate him to the fullest development of the mind. It is the Christian alone who is in touch with the fountain of truth. In this age as in the preceding ones, the Christian teacher is the only safe one." "Daily intercourse with Christian teachers," was for McCrimmon the most "potent influence" for making students good moral citizens — even those who refused to become Christians.

Yet Christian education had more to it than the development of individual strengths within an evangelical environment. As far as McCrimmon was concerned, "The Christian college not only teaches how to develop the life but also instructs how to give that life for the benefit of mankind." He concluded his address on a powerful nationalistic note:

When we view the opportunity before us our hearts warm with enthusiasm and inspiration. The desire to serve our country and our God, comes with ever increasing power. We are Canadians and we wish to see in Canada the highest type of manhood. Let us do our best to cultivate its people to nobility of character and purity of life. Let us grow them large because they are capable of such growth. Let us catch the sentiments of Dean Stanley when he said, "The heroes of mankind are the mountains, the highlands of the moral world. They diversify the monotony. They furnish the water shed of its history." The highest, holiest manhood must ever be our ideal.

For McCrimmon, Baptist education had a special role to play in creating Canadian "moral giants" — men and women who would tower over their contemporaries and be as "Cities upon the Hill" pointing in the direction of the New Jerusalem.

As chancellor of McMaster, from 1911 to 1922, McCrimmon attempted to implement what he called his "missionary conception" of higher education. He often would refer to the evangelical Baptist "view of Christian Education which has led many of the men who have joined the staff of our colleges to leave even the pastorate that they might weave their Christian influence into the lives of developing young men and women destined in different callings in life."[46] For McCrimmon, until his death, "The Christian college is the natural and inevitable complement to the Christian home, the church and the Sunday school. The state schools are worthy of all praise as they direct students to the truth, but after all any truth is unrelated truth, is truth without its meaning for life, until it is centred in Christ, the Son of God and the God of truth."[47]

For Baptists, however, just any Christian college would not do. It would have to be a Baptist institution because of what McCrimmon felt was the crucial significance of the denominational "matrix" in Christian education.[48] He stressed the fact that "our mission in education is with the adolescent in the uncertain years of his youth when he is trying out his tentatives, striving in this direction and that, criticizing his social and religious relations, seeking his ideals, discovering his life-work." It was therefore incumbent upon the Ontario and Quebec Baptist Convention to thrust

Christ at the centre of [McMaster] life . . . so that His creative personality may organize and direct the developing powers; that to accomplish this purpose there are required Christian teachers, Christian conditions, continuous action of these personalities and conditions, and freedom to exercise such influences; that to furnish this continuous exercise of Christian influence, there must be adequate control so that there may be as great a guarantee as possible respecting the character of the teachers and the conditions; that as a Baptist denomination we must act consistently with our principles, or not act at all.[49]

For McCrimmon, these "principles" were obviously contained in McMaster University's 1887 Act of Incorporation.

He proudly described in 1920 the McMaster he had helped shape into what he called a leading "Christian University in this Canada of ours."[50] At McMaster, the unique Baptist blend of pietism, soul liberty, and missionary outreach greatly influenced each student "every day." The university, moreover,

furnishes him with Christian teachers chosen because they are members of evangelical churches; it indoctrinates him with the principles of scholarship and civilization efficiently; it furnishes him with an atmosphere in which it is the natural and customary procedure to attend Church service; it gives the student a broad course of liberal culture in which to find himself and his sphere of work and at the same time gives an introduction to specialization ... there is no thought too strenuous for its activity, no freedom too great for its chastened democracy; it is conducive to the cohesiveness and solidarity of our denomination and renders it a more effective fighting unit in the church militant; it furnishes ... Christian leaders ... it turns the thoughts of its Arts students to the ministry to keep them within calling distance; ... it complements from a religious standpoint and under religious influences, the home, the church and the Sunday school, and at the same time complements from the educational standpoint the other universities of Canada.[51]

McMaster, in theory and in practice, was emphatically not an introverted, morbidly introspective, and defensive Baptist bible college. Rather, it was a small Christian university, open to new scholarship, concerned with the preservation of Christian truth, but always within the context of "liberal culture." It, obviously, had the best of both worlds — orthodox evangelicalism on the one hand and "strenuous thought" and specialization on the other. McCrimmon sincerely believed that he could energize McMaster with the potent mix of orthodoxy and innovation. Instead of energizing the institution, however, and using it to strengthen the Convention, in the 1920s McCrimmon saw his beloved McMaster University help precipitate a furious denominational civil war, from which the Convention has still not yet fully recovered.

The first World War threatened to destroy McCrimmon's McMaster even before T.T. Shields endeavoured to accomplish this end in the 1920s. Despite a myriad of external and internal problems, McCrimmon successfully steered his institution through the war years. In doing so, his already fragile health suffered and he found himself without the necessary physical and mental strength to deal constructively with the renewed and even more bitter fundamentalist-modernist controversy that engulfed the Convention at McMaster during the years immediately following the end of hostilities. McCrimmon, in 1920, felt compelled to inform his dean of Arts that "owing to the persistent character of my sleeplessness and the fiendish delight it takes in making me super-nervous over the most trivial matters it was best that no further University correspondence should be sent to me."[52] The chancellor was immobilized. In 1921 the Senate began to look for a replacement and the next year Howard Primrose Whidden was named the new chancellor.

McCrimmon's illness may have had both physiological and psychological roots. He saw his idealized McMaster being transformed before his very eyes; the small "Christian university" intent upon making good pious Baptists was being transformed by the forces of change unleashed by the war into an increasingly secular institution of higher learning. Science and the social sciences were replacing Christian orthodoxy as the primary moulders of student minds. McCrimmon found himself increasingly isolated. His conservative theology pushed him in the direction of fundamentalists like T.T. Shields — people he instinctively disliked because of their spiritual hubris, their violent language, and their vociferous alienation from Canadian cultural norms. McCrimmon's deep concern about education and learning pushed him towards those liberal Christians who were increasingly committed to intellectual accommodation at the expense of orthodoxy. It is not surprising that McCrimmon was immobilized in 1920 and 1921, incapable of providing leadership and direction to his much troubled Convention and university.

On his retirement from the chancellorship, McCrimmon returned to teaching at McMaster. He was president of the Baptist Convention of Ontario and Quebec for three terms between 1921 and 1932, and he also served as vice-president of the Baptist World Alliance. When he died in 1935, McCrimmon was still teaching at McMaster — now located in Hamilton — where he had seen his small Baptist university transformed into a largely secular university and into an academic outpost of the new industrial order.[53]

Abraham Lincoln McCrimmon's obituary in the *Canadian Baptist* on 25 April 1935 captured the man as well as any contemporary analysis. According to the *Canadian Baptist*

the deep secret of his life was found in Christ. That was the centre he sought for himself and to that centre he sought to lead others ... He rejoiced in the intimations and certainties of immortality. How he loved in his classroom discussions to speak of the lines that went out into the unseen. His faith in his Saviour was as simple and humble as that of a child. In that faith he lived nobly, he laboured fruitfully, and he died triumphantly.

Such an obituary could never have been written about H.P. Whidden when he died in 1952. In fact, when his successor, G.P. Gilmour, wrote Whidden's official "Tribute," there was a remarkable absence of any references to spiritual and religious gifts and attributes. After discussing briefly Whidden's successful defence at McMaster during the turbulent 1920s, Gilmour maintained that:

Graduates remember Howard Primrose Whidden chiefly as a man of striking appearance, unusual dignity and broad educational outlook. A goodly number of them remember him as a helpful personal friend, for he had a gift for friendship and became the confidant and adviser of many... His staff knew him as a man who chose men and women with care, who inspired faith in the work of a small university, and who guided them more by gentle hints and wise suggestions than by orders or interference.[54]

Whidden was born in Antigonish, Nova Scotia in 1870; after graduating from Acadia University in 1891 he studied theology at McMaster where he received his BD degree in 1894. He did further graduate work at the University of Chicago and then served as a Baptist minister in Morden, Manitoba and Galt, Ontario. In 1900 he was appointed professor of English and biblical literature at Brandon College. Three years later he accepted a call to the prestigious Northern Baptist Convention Church in Dayton, Ohio, where he served for almost nine years before returning in 1912 to Brandon as its president. He left Brandon in 1923 for McMaster. It should also be noted that he served as a Union member of Parliament from 1917 to 1921.

Whidden, as the *Winnipeg Tribune* correctly observed on 28 June 1939, was very "cool" and "suave" and handled pressure extremely well. "No matter how sharply he differed" from his critics "one never saw him ruffled to the point of sarcasm and unkindness in debate."[55] He was, without question, a consummate academic politician. A close friend and president of the University of Western Ontario, W. Sherwood Fox, once wrote that Whidden had, since his early Brandon days, "revealed a natural flair for administration and the handling of people."[56] And as far as Fox was concerned in 1941, Whidden had been chosen as McMaster's chancellor in 1922 because of his administrative gifts and not because of his spirituality. In fact, the evidence suggests that Whidden had definitely moved from a conservative evangelical position in the late 1890s to a liberal Christian position in the 1920s — far beyond McCrimmon's conservative evangelicalism.

A persistent and persuasive advocate of modernity and progress, and closely associated with the Ontario business elite, an active Mason and a committed Conservative, Whidden was perceived by many members of McMaster's Board of Governors — many of whom were key members of the Canadian business elite — as just the man to lead the university out of the dark forests of theological backwardness into the mainstream of North American bourgeois success and respectability. He was in so many ways the perfect "organic intellectual" determined to win the support of the traditional Canadian Baptists in what Gramsci has called "the new social, economic and political order." McCrimmon, who had tried to walk the knife edge between the nineteenth century and the twentieth — by finding his theological bearings in a distant past — had failed to solve McMaster's problems. Moreover, he was profoundly suspicious of various aspects of capitalism and consumerism. Perhaps, Whidden could influence McMaster positively, not by looking backwards but forward — his vision unencumbered either by embarrassing evangelical outcroppings or by seemingly outmoded rural values.

Whidden's insensitivity to the fundamentalist criticism of McMaster's apparent move towards modernism in the 1920s undoubtedly played a key role in bringing about the bitter split in the Convention.

Whidden, of course, was not responsible for the split. A myriad of complex forces merged in the mid 1920s to bring it about.[57] Yet, he could have done more to placate the fundamentalists — but probably not enough. Perhaps only the replacement of Whidden by Shields would have persuaded the followers of Shields to remain in the Convention.

As might have been expected, Whidden said little and wrote little about Christian higher education. He, evidently, was far more interested in getting things actually done at McMaster than in talking about what might be done. He was always a pragmatic Nova Scotian far more concerned with present realities than with theories spinning off into the imagination.

In his inaugural address given in November 1923, Chancellor Whidden clearly revealed how his philosophy of education differed from that of his predecessor. It was a very brief address, and one of the few available statements that Whidden ever published about education.[58] There were only eleven brief paragraphs in Whidden's speech.[59] The first seven dealt with his predecessors, McVicar, Rand, Wallace, McKay and McCrimmon. There was also a passing mention of the "fine Christian idealism" and "rugged confidence" of Senator William McMaster. Then Whidden very briefly discussed what he referred to as the "Certain Essentials of Liberal Education." The word Christian or the word Christ was not even referred to once in the body of the new chancellor's speech. It was Whidden's contention that:

The chief business of the smaller university is to furnish a liberal education. If, as Kant said, 'Man's greatest concern is to know how he shall properly fill his place in the universe and understand what he must be in order to be a man,' then education is, as Galsworthy recently said, the sacred concern, indeed the only hope of the nation. *Liberal education should seek to relate the individual to his universe.* I refer more especially to the universe of things. Think of all that nature has in store for those who are willing to learn the simple yet sublime laws of nature.

It is noteworthy that Whidden underscored only one sentence in the first section of his speech. *"Liberal education should seek to relate the individual to the universe."* No mention was made of McMaster's motto "In Christ All Things Consist." No mention, moreover, was made of "Truth" being "centred in Christ." And Whidden was strangely silent about any special aspect of Christian education — either narrowly or broadly defined.

After discussing generally the rise of "the great newer sciences … Physics … Chemistry, Biology and Geology," Whidden suddenly declared "Through these four the modern world has largely become what it is." He then went on:

As a result of the application of scientific knowledge the stellar spaces have been measured and brought near, the subtle forces hidden in air and earth and sea have been harnessed and made to serve man's need. The whole development and structure of material things in past ages is brought within our ken; the life of plant and animal is so much better understood that human life is conserved in previously unthought of ways. In connection with all this there has gone on steadily an emancipation of the mind of man with regard to the dominance of the material.

Thus, for Whidden, the "newer sciences," not the Bible, not Christ, not fundamentalism, had brought about the modern "emancipation of the mind." Scientific knowledge and not evangelical orthodoxy — and not even experiential Christianity — had led to true freedom — the "emancipation of the mind."

Even though he did not expect that the "newer sciences" would produce great specialists at McMaster, Whidden, nevertheless, hoped that they would produce intelligent students aware of the basic rudiments of "modern scientific" life. But Whidden, building a bridge in his argument to other areas of the university, agreed with Tyndell that "it is not through science, nor through literature that human nature is made whole, but through a fusion of both." He developed this argument a little further:

We see then how natural it is to urge that in a truly liberal educational programme recognition be given to the study of universal things in human life. *The mind of youth must be brought into sympathetic acquaintance with the best there is in the experience of man.* There is still need for the classics as well as for modern language and literature. If the coming leaders of thought and action are to know the best that has been thought or said in other days, the old humanities must not be thrown to the discard.

In the second part of his inaugural address, Whidden underlined one other sentence — a sentence he must have regarded as being especially heavy with meaning. *"The mind of youth"* he stressed *"must be brought into sympathetic acquaintance with the best there is in the experience of man."* Whidden had thrown his knowledge net over the entire "experience of man" — not only a tiny section of it — and had urged all of his teachers to bring their students "into sympathetic acquaintance" with the best there was in the "experience of man."

McMaster's sixth chancellor then concluded his address with a call for a greater interest and awareness of the "New Humanities." "The historical, social and political sciences," he asserted, "must be more vitally understood and set forth if we are rightly to orient the student into his world of citizenship."

As Whidden came down from the platform after giving his inaugural address, he was confronted by one of T.T. Shields' lieutenants with a bitter complaint from his chief, not about the address, but about the honorary degree the university had granted to Dr. William H.P. Faunce, the president of Brown University, and a person Shields regarded as an unreconstructed modernist. The "Faunce Controversy" simmered into 1924 when, at the convention of that year, Whidden actually seconded a Shields' motion that "this Convention relies upon the Senate to exercise care that honourary degrees be not conferred upon religious leaders whose theological views are known to be out of harmony with the cardinal principles of evangelical Christianity."[60] After being re-elected to the Board of Governors of McMaster University by the 1924 Convention, Shields was absolutely certain that he, at last, had the Convention modernists on the run. And, in particular, he felt that he had cowed Whidden into submission. Shields, however, not for the first time in his life, had completely misread not only the general theological situation but also the new chancellor.

Much to Shields' disgust, on 25 July 1925 the McMaster Senate endorsed the appointment of L.H. Marshall to the Chair of pastoral theology. As far as Shields was concerned, the English Baptist theologian Marshall was a modernist and his appointment was convincing proof that Whidden and his supporters had abandoned evangelical principles. Eventually, the "Marshall Controversy" resulted in a major split in the denomination and in late 1926 Shields and hundreds of supporters angrily quit the Convention.[61]

It is sometimes forgotten that during the first three decades of the twentieth century T.T. Shields probably had a greater impact — however negative — upon McMaster University than did any other person. A catalyst for denominational schism and theological warfare, Shields was either loved or hated, respected or detested. There was no middle ground for those who knew the extraordinarily gifted fundamentalist preacher and polemicist. One of his early disciples — Dr. Morley Hall — superbly captured this polarizing tendency in a story he once told about two women in the Jarvis Street Baptist Church who were struck by the special effect of a shaft of morning sunshine on the countenance of the Reverend Shields as he piously sat behind his pulpit. "One was impressed by the angelic look on her pastor's face," Hall recounted. "The other was certain that she saw traces of the demonic."[62] In 1931, Jean Graham, a perceptive *Saturday Night* reporter, also captured the almost Janus-like quality of Shields:

Could this gentleman of benign countenance and mellifluous voice be the turbulent pastor who hated his enemies and loathed his theological opponents until he became wrathy and violent and longed for the Lord to destroy them? Surely there must be some mistake. As the sermon progressed the bewilderment increased. It was what would be called a simple gospel sermon, with no reference to modernists or other monstrosities ... During the week following he appeared to go on a rampage of malice, hatred and uncharitableness. Who is the true Dr. Shields? Is he the kindly Christian or the peevish propagandist?[63]

Shields, it seems clear, was, in fact, both. He was an extraordinary mix of opposites — of love and hate, of gentleness and harshness, of sensibility and callousness. He was referred to by his enemies as "a dictator," as "a hypocrite," as "vain and egotistical," and as a "man without a Christian heart."[64] His friends, however, regarded him as a "man of God," "devastatingly honest" and absolutely "selfless."

Thomas Todhunter Shields was born in Bristol, England, in 1873, the fifth of eight children. His father, originally an Anglican priest, was eventually ordained a Baptist minister and emigrated with his family, in 1888, to pastor a small Baptist church in western Ontario. T.T. Shields, after his conversion in his father's church in 1891, was ordained a Baptist minister "without the benefit of either a college or a seminary education."[65] After serving a number of Baptist churches in western Ontario, T.T. Shields, in 1910, was called to the prestigious Jarvis Street pastorate. He remained there until his death in 1955.

A brilliant preacher, widely regarded as the "Spurgeon of Canada" since at least the first decade of the twentieth century, Shields had had serious reservations about McMaster University's special role within the Baptist denomination. Overly sensitive to his own lack of seminary training, he resented the way McMaster theology graduates leapfrogged into large urban churches over the careers of their less well educated fellow ministers. According to Shields, in his controversial book *The Plot That Failed*,

Certain officials of McMaster University... had come to regard the Baptist denomination as McMaster's special preserve. Non-McMaster men were tolerated for the doing of rough work, even as the Chinese coolies were used to do rough work on the Western Front in the Great War. Train loads of coolies passed through Canada. But no one ever supposed that one of them could by any possibility become colonel of a regiment, or commander of a brigade, or of an army, to say nothing of the possibility of one's carrying a field-marshal's baton in his knapsack. To my personal knowledge certain of the Faculty of McMaster looked upon non-McMaster men as useful for preparing dugouts, lighting fires, and perhaps for carrying meals to the Graduates of McMaster University.[66]

Shields, however, did not explain in *The Plot That Failed* how he had become "commander" and "field-marshal" at Jarvis Street despite McMaster's policy of regarding, as he put it, "The Denomination" as its own "great estate."[67] Nor did Shields explain why he had been awarded an honorary DD by McMaster in 1918.

Shields' view of Christian education in the North American context underwent significant change in the 1920s. This point is sometimes not taken into account by scholars who merely see him as a closed minded fundamentalist whose views of all issues had clicked into firm place by the turn of the century. From 1922 to 1925, for example, Shields was sharply ambivalent about McMaster's educational role. Despite his criticism of the denominational imperialism of the institution, nevertheless until at least 1925 Shields still felt that there was some hope for the institution, provided that Baptist fundamentalists were appointed to its theological department. The "Marshall Controversy" of 1925, however, provided Shields with convincing proof that the university and the denomination had irrevocably abandoned its orthodox Christian traditions and had, moreover, destroyed any remaining fundamentalist "hope" for theological renewal and spiritual revitalization.

In the 21 September 1922 issue of the *Gospel Witness*, Shields began his public discussion of McMaster University and Christian educa-tion. In a major article entitled "What About McMaster University?" Shields raised the question of whether the non-theology part of McMaster was, in any way, "serving the Denomination?" His response was that there was an unanswerable argument for a sepa-rate independent Baptist university but only if in such an institution "vital and vigorous Baptist principles" permeated the teaching of all courses. If such was not the case, he felt, it made a great deal of pedagogical and financial sense for Baptist students in arts and sci-ence to be sent to secular universities rather than McMaster. The large sums of money saved by the denomination would be far better used to support a vibrant, biblically based seminary.

In other articles in the *Gospel Witness* published late in 1922, Shields developed further his ideas concerning Christian education. For him

The Baptist view is that a Christian is a Christian everywhere, and in all things; that if a man confesses that Jesus Christ is his Lord, his subjection to Christ will color even his thinking, and that then, no matter what subject he may teach, whether it be history, or science, or language, or literature, or psychology, or sociology, or political economy, or theology he will view everything from a Christian standpoint, and there will be a savor of Christ in all his teaching: and his devotion to Christ will compound the principles of the gospel into a precious nard which will become diffused by His pre-sence until the house is filled with the odor of the ointment: and the very atmosphere becomes charged with spiritual vitality.[68]

As had been the case with A.L. McCrimmon in 1920, Shields endorsed the view that the evangelical ideal of Christian education could, in fact, be realized at McMaster. And he, therefore, argued that any move toward "federation with the Provincial University" was "a retrograde step" and all Baptists were urged to "prevent it at all possible cost."[69]

Shields would stress over and over again in late 1922 that McCrimmon's successor as chancellor at McMaster had to make the arts and science faculty into a "Baptist missionary educational institution,"[70] where students were not only converted to evangelical Christianity but also persuaded to sacrifice their lives and careers for their Saviour. The appointment of Whidden, a man distrusted by Shields, seemed to provide convincing evidence to the Jarvis Street pastor that his ideal Christian institution would never be realized at McMaster. Consequently, in May 1923, he began to attack McMaster University because the "absolutely anti-Christian... doctrine of Evolution" was being taught there.[71] As Shields moved more and more into the premillennial camp in 1923, his criticism of McMaster intensified; and the Faunce honorary degree in November 1923, gave him the excuse to denounce Whidden and the Senate for abandoning "the faith once delivered to the saints."[72] By early January 1924, Shields was organizing special prayer meetings for McMaster University. At these, he announced to the readers of the *Gospel Witness* on 17 January:

We shall ask the Lord to arise in His might and by His own power to deliver the University out of the hands of those whose principles have blighted the denomination for so long, and to deliver it to the management of those who will be true to "the faith once for all delivered to the Saints."... We who profess to believe in the supernatural must put our profession to the proof by invoking supernatural power to fight our battles.

One month later Shields viciously attacked Whidden as the man responsible for the remarkable growth of modernism at Brandon College. And Shields warned his readers that the new chancellor of McMaster had also "encouraged" this "kind of teaching" at the Toronto institution.[73]

By November 1924, Shields' views about McMaster had changed, yet again. Encouraged by the Convention's endorsement of his criticism of the Faunce honorary degree and his contention that such degrees should not be "conferred upon religious leaders whose theological views are known to be out of harmony with the cardinal principles of evangelical Christianity,"[74] he resolved to give McMaster and the Convention another last chance. The other Shields — apparently seeking compromise — suddenly appeared from the bitter, bloody, internecine theological civil war.

Shields informed his shocked Toronto Baptist fundamentalist associates on 4 November 1924 that he was genuinely "sorry" if any of his anti-McMaster statements had, in fact, "hurt anyone."[75] He told them that he had

given our hand to the Chancellor [Whidden] as the representative of our educational work; and we are prepared to trust him, to follow him, and to rely (to use the term in the resolution which we moved and which he seconded) upon him to carry out in spirit and letter and we all know to be the Convention's desire. We therefore in this public way ... [Shields expected that his letter would be immediately published in the *Gospel Witness*] pledge our heart and hand to the support of our educational work.[76]

All of a sudden, Shields was now sympathetically describing McMaster as "our educational work." He obviously felt that the 1924 Convention had endorsed his fundamentalist position and that he was therefore in an unprecedented position to gain control, once and for all, over the strategically significant institution — McMaster University. He looked forward to the day when his McMaster men would make the old McMaster graduates "coolies" and "servants" of the fundamentalist elite.

In early November 1924, a euphoric Shields confidently expressed his new vision of "Christian Education." He first asserted that McMaster, as a Christian university, had "to resemble other universities" in conforming "to the highest standards of scholarship." But it had to be more than this as well. "Our view of the ideal for McMaster," Shields contended, "is not that it should be like the State University-minus — but like the State University-plus." And for him the plus was the orthodox Christian dynamic. And this dynamic would be provided not only by committed evangelical faculty at McMaster, in arts, science and theology, but by a new "Baptist Bible Training College" administratively "in connection with McMaster University." Such a bible college, Shields contended, would transform McMaster. "It would bring to its halls," he went on,

hundreds of young people who would live every day, not with books about the Bible, but with the Bible itself. It would bring to the University a still more spiritual atmosphere than now obtains ... for it is impossible that a great host of young people should engage in the study of God's word without filling the place with prayer and praise. Thus McMaster University would become more than ever a centre of evangelical teaching and evangelistic enthusiasm and effort.[77]

Shields was convinced that the bible school, which he hoped would be associated in an intimate way with his own church, would strengthen and not weaken McMaster University. At the "Bible Training School," he argued, hundreds of students would "enlarge their minds" and thus be "inspire[d] ... with a desire for higher learning" as they "would naturally pass from the Bible course of the College into the regular university courses." Such a bible school, Shields prophesied, would encourage the fundamentalist Baptists, in particular, to "give the University a place in the[ir] hearts and ... prayers ... such as nothing else would do." He knew of many ministers, including himself, who would offer their services to the school at "a nominal cost." Shields then concluded with the declaration that it was incumbent upon his supporters to

set up a standard of Christian learning which may be used to enlighten even those who count themselves wise. In other words, our duty is not to follow the example of other universities in these dark days but to set up a new standard of absolute loyalty to truth as revealed in Him who in all things consist. Hence, it is our duty to evangelize the rationalist university and to teach the rationalist scholar.[78]

Shields' proposal, as might have been expected, fell on deaf Convention ears. It was perceived as a fundamentalist Trojan Horse to capture McMaster for the Shields' forces. And even Shields, by the summer of 1925, had lost his enthusiasm for it. Moving inexorably towards schism, he proposed in late August a month after the Marshall appointment, to establish his own independent "Toronto Baptist Pastors College" based upon what he referred to as "the New Testament ... educational ideal." "Christ must be put first," he declared in direct opposition to the liberal platitudes of Whidden's inaugural address. "The end of all education," Shields asserted, echoing McCrimmon, was "to know Him [the Christ] better." All true learning automatically centred on "a better knowledge of Christ."

A pursuit of such an ideal can be maintained only in a healthy spiritual atmosphere. A man is not likely to develop an aesthetic taste in a coal mine; it is not probable that one would grow as a musician amid the din of a boiler making establishment. So to keep always in view this worthiest of all ideals, one must not only be possessed of a vigorous spiritual health himself but his soul must breathe the atmosphere of the heavenly places in Christ. Hence we believe that such an ideal is most likely to be realized in association with a New Testament church, founded upon New Testament principles, surcharged with the power of the Holy Spirit.[79]

Such a church was of course available — Jarvis Street Baptist Church — and here at his church and at his college the students would have their faith built up and not destroyed. The "Bible" would be "The Principal Text Book" and learning to preach the evangelistic gospel, the only practical course. All faculty members were to be "required to subscribe" to the fundamentalist "Confession of Faith of the Baptist Bible Union of North America... publicly at the beginning of each term."[80] If they attempted to qualify in any way, any of these fundamentalist tenets, they would be immediately fired. Belonging to a so-called evangelical church was not enough; only a yearly fundamentalist litmus test, administered by Shields, would do.

Early in 1926, the Toronto Baptist Seminary opened its doors to its first students. A short time before, Shields had announced to his supporters that he was "at war" with McMaster and the Convention. Their "moderate Modernism" — as he spitefully called it — and their "spirit of the Spanish Inquisition" had compelled him to implement in the new year his August 1925 "College plan." He equated so-called "Baptist liberty" with a "mild attack of small pox or of leprosy."[81] By January 1927, Shields had organized his followers into a separate Baptist organization, the Regular Baptist Missionary and Educational Society of Canada. A short time later this body was reorganized as "the Union of Regular Baptist Churches of Ontario and Quebec."[82]

Thus by 1927, Shields and his supporters had their own seminary, their own separate "Union," their own newspaper, the *Gospel Witness*, which had been started in 1922. They, therefore, possessed a smoothly running parallel Baptist organization to compete with their Convention opponents. And by May 1927, Shields had a university to compete with McMaster — Des Moines University, in Iowa — a financially troubled institution taken over by the fundamentalist Bible Baptist Union of North America, of which organization Shields was president from 1923 to 1930. Unable to put things right at McMaster, Shields enthusiastically turned to the task of transforming Des Moines into what McMaster had refused to be: "a great Christian institution of higher learning... absolutely free from the taint of modernism."[83]

But within two years, the Des Moines experiment had proven to be an embarrassing failure as a student revolt and a bitter American reaction against the anglophile Shields resulted in the closing of the university.[84] What happened with Des Moines University, a fundamentalist Baptist university which Shields ruled with an iron hand, might have also happened with McMaster, if Shields had had his way. During the period when Shields' Des Moines experiment was disintegrating into disaster, Whidden was carefully consolidating his position at McMaster and preparing the way for a move to Hamilton. In 1928, after much discussion, "The 'New McMaster Campaign' was launched which resulted two years later in the physical re-establishment" of McMaster in the west end of the "Steel City."[85] Whidden must have been delighted to have escaped the presence of Shields and also the bitter memories of what one of his associates referred to as "a lovely war."[86] He also must have been pleased to have been given the opportunity to build *his* kind of Baptist university. If he had lived to see the day when in 1957, the Convention cut its official ties with McMaster Univeristy and was content with the creation of McMaster Divinity College, Whidden would have been ecstatic indeed. This was the way he was leading McMaster when he led the move to Hamilton in 1930. Whidden would have agreed with his close friend John Gilmour, that "McMaster had only narrowly escaped being a glorified Woodstock rather than a university."[87] McCrimmon's McMaster and also that of Shields was obviously a "glorified Woodstock" — a Baptist bible college. The new McMaster, according to Whidden, must have been a real university — a place where the intellectual "deputies" of the new dominant class could help to impose on their society hegemonic control and order.

WALTER E. ELLIS

What the Times Demand: Brandon College and Baptist Higher Education in Western Canada

In June 1857, the cornerstone of the Canadian Literary Institute was laid in Woodstock, Ontario, an occasion hailed by the Grand River North Baptist Association the following year because "the progress of science and the march of intellect demands that we keep pace with the times we live in if we are not to be left behind."[1] Similarly, at the annual meetings of the Baptist Home Mission Convention of Manitoba and the North-West in 1883, in the presence of Professor Malcolm MacVicar of McMaster Hall, Toronto, and representatives of the American Baptist Publication Society, the fledgling Baptist denomination on the prairies resolved that "in view of the intelligent and enterprising classes from the Eastern Provinces and other countries," the excellent school system of Manitoba, and the establishment of university and denominational colleges in Winnipeg, circumstances demanded that Baptists "keep pace with the Spirit of the times [and] establish a college in Winnipeg."[2]

Keeping pace with the times for Baptists in the west meant catching up with the other denominations. In 1877, the provincial government approved legislation to establish the University of Manitoba as the exclusive degree granting institution in the province. In effect, it was a central examination agency for the extant denominational colleges, Manitoba (Presbyterian), Wesley (Methodist), St. Johns' (Anglican), and St. Boniface (Roman Catholic). This posed a problem for Baptists. Historically, the Baptists held that the function of civil government was purely and always secular, and their struggle for institutional independence in Ontario would profoundly affect their attitude to higher education in Western Canada as well.

Several factors had inhibited Baptist missionary and educational enterprises on the western frontier and prevented their arrival until 1873. Among these were the often bitter denominational divisions in central Canada produced by theological disputes — Calvinists as opposed to Arminians — advocates of open communion battling those advocating communion only for immersed Baptist Church members. But of even greater significance was a lack of consensus on higher education policy. Baptist populists had an inherent distrust of elitist education, especially for the "making of ministers." Whether Baptists should federate with state universities, duplicate liberal arts programs offered in secular institutions, limit their educational enterprises to the teaching of theology, or offer arts and theology together in the same institution, were the central, key issues.

In 1879, the theology department of the Canadian Literary Institute at Woodstock had been moved to Toronto and the Toronto Baptist College founded with philanthropic assistance from Senator William McMaster. Over the next seven years, under the influence of the Reverend John Howard Castle, Malcolm MacVicar, and Susan Moulton McMaster, steps were taken which culminated on 22 April 1887 in the chartering of McMaster University as an independent university empowered to grant degrees. The movement to consolidate arts and theological education on a coeducational basis in Toronto would leave a bitter taste in the mouth of many Woodstock supporters and many Baptist democrats.

It was part of the same agenda that brought Malcolm MacVicar to the 1883 Manitoba and North-West Convention. He was there because of the collapse of Prairie College, Rapid City, Manitoba, to persuade western Baptists to join the maritimes in transferring theological education to Toronto Baptist College.

Tensions ran high as the assembly at Portage La Prairie convened. Upon the death of Dr. R.A. Fyfe, the founder of the Canadian Literary Institute in 1878, his aging colleague, the Reverend John Crawford, previously pastor at Cheltenham and a powerful postmillennial Baptist, determined to join the western migration and establish an institute (subsequently named Prairie College) for the training of ministers on the frontier. Aided by the Reverend G.B. Davis, Crawford hoped to combine education with evangelism "to meet the incoming population of the prairies with the Gospel of Jesus Christ and to establish churches among them."[3] Students were to home-stead in summer and study mostly in the winter months, because Crawford "believed in manual training in education."[4]

The first contingent of students arrived in Rapid City, on 23 March, the second, on 9 July 1880. William Davis had secured 1,100 acres for the seminary. Land was cleared, crops planted, and a three storey stone building finished before winter. Eighteen students studied at Prairie College as snow fell. Their efforts included founding a literary society and a college paper.

In 1881 Professor S.J. McKee, an associate of Crawford at Woodstock, arrived at Rapid City to organize the Rapid City Academy. He was accompanied by Professor J.E. Wells, soon to become editor of the *Rapid City Standard*. True to the Baptist educa-tional philosophy that prevailed in Ontario prior to 1880, the academy would complement, not compete with, the seminary because it would enrol literary students, whereas "Prairie College, on the hill accepted only students for theology on the manual labor basis."[5]

The boom year of 1881 was followed by a bust in land speculation, due in part to the fact that transport of agricultural produce to the east remained difficult. Funds pledged by the Prairie College Missio-nary Society did not materialize, and differences between Crawford and William Davis added to a growing crisis.

MacVicar's arrival at the 1883 Convention was providential. Prairie College would close. Its students, along with theology students from Acadia, would be educated at Toronto Baptist College. Seven of the thirteen Prairie College students took the option. The others transfer-red to Manitoba College (Presbyterian) or travelled to Moody Bible Institute in Chicago. McKee's Rapid City Academy would continue to educate "literary students."

Explaining the closing of Prairie College, J.B. McArthur and A.A. Cameron — a Baptist minister located in Winnipeg — held that "the North-West had outgrown the college. The intelligent classes which made their homes here demanded a school of a higher grade than the resources of its treasury could sustain." Besides, the "farm man-agement was a serious incumbrance!"[6]

Baptists on the prairies would soon rue their decision. As John E. Davis succinctly reported, "very little progress was made by Baptists in Manitoba for the next 8 years."[7] Acquiescence in the grand design of Toronto Baptists resulted in students going east or south never to return.

In consequence, in September 1885, a verbal broadside was shot by A.A. Cameron who complained that eastern Baptists had spent $1,250,000 in the interests of an educated ministry. "We do not say lessen the ministerial sails, but we do say that with all this sail the Baptist ship must be made to carry more Home Mission cargo for ballast," he asserted.[8]

Meantime, prairie Baptists watched in dismay the machinations related to the founding of McMaster University and the dismemberment of Woodstock College. Even as McMaster began, the *North-West Baptist* bluntly warned, "Rival banners are being hoisted in Woodstock and Toronto and around them the forces of our denomination are rallying." This was inimical to western interests. Truth was that the Dominion Board of Missions located in Toronto was deeply interested, not in Manitoba Home missions, but "in our educational institutions... at the sacrifice of our Baptist churches east and west."[9]

Western disenchantment was spurred by news in 1890 that "all the students both of Toronto and Woodstock [would] be needed for mission work in Ontario and Quebec."[10] At this juncture, A.A. Cameron, the articulate exponent of western concerns, resigned from First Baptist Church, Winnipeg, to accept the call to the First Baptist Church of Denver. He left a constituency increasingly convinced that only an indigenous solution would resolve their priority need of pastoral leadership.

The initial proposal was to provide quarters for young men at Rapid City where the academy would teach the basic three "r's" when required, and offer introductions to biblical and language studies. However, the logic of proximity to higher education in Winnipeg prevailed and in November 1890, sixteen students enrolled at Grant College under the tutelage of Mr Edward Duff of Peterborough and the dynamic Reverend Alexander Grant of First Baptist Church, Winnipeg. Duff's ill health and subsequent death, the contiguity of Manitoba College, and a $700 financial deficit resulted in closing of the bible college after one year. Thus, the experiment in urban studies modelled after Spurgeon's College, London, met a similar fate as Prairie College, the rural populist experiment.[11]

Faced with a population explosion, but a drought of pastors, the *North-West Baptist* in 1893 questioned the priorities and goals of McMaster University and the Toronto Baptist elite. Assurances from the noted McMaster church historian, A.H. Newman, that in ten years the number of "equipped ministers" would increase fivefold were rudely dismissed. "Ten years forsooth!" Manitoba could not wait "ten years." There was not a solitary graduate of McMaster west of the Great Lakes, not one professor on her Toronto faculty that knew by contact a thing about the frontier. "We want *MEN*, graduates or no graduates, arts or no arts, theology or no theology, men who are prepared to cope with the difficulties of the work, and we have a right to ask and intend to keep asking what are the prospects of getting them, and getting them without delay," asserted the editor, the Reverend Alexander Grant, whose blunt insinuations that McMaster produced dandies and not "Men" may well have been missed by the eastern establishment.[12]

In the meantime, McKee continued to expand his academy in Rapid City. However, in 1881, the Canadian Pacific Railway chose Brandon as a divisional point. In consequence, Brandon grew while Rapid City languished. Finally, in 1889, the school was transferred twenty miles south and renamed Brandon Academy. That same year Baptists were encouraged when reports surfaced that Brandon citizens were prepared to raise $10,000 in support of a college. In response, the Manitoba and North-West Baptist Assembly passed a resolution that, provided $8,500 could be realized for triennial expenses, they would comply because they were convinced that "a first class educational institution" was necessary in Manitoba. Their priorities were clear. It would provide "... needed training (a) for our students for the ministry, and (b) for boys and girls from Baptist families, who are compelled to leave home to obtain an education."[13]

However, the project was summarily aborted when the deputation sent east in search of funds reported in August 1890, that due to the Grande Ligne Mission Drive — to support Baptist work among French Canadians — aid from Ontario and Quebec Baptists had been refused. They reported that the general feeling in the east was that there was a lack of unity on education plans in western Canada.

In 1898 the Manitoba Baptist Convention again appointed a committee to consider expansion of McKee's Academy into a Baptist college and it proposed that the arts department affiliate with the

University of Manitoba and the theology department with McMaster. Finally, in July 1899, the Convention Assembly approved a recommendation that "the Manitoba Convention proceed to inaugurate a denominational school at once; that Dr A.P. McDiarmid be appointed principal; and that the twenty-one member Board of Directors choose the college site."[14]

Prairie Baptists were optimistic. Dr A.P. McDiarmid, a graduate in philosophy from the University of Toronto and Rochester Seminary had teaching and administrative skills and proper connections among influential eastern and American Baptists. Support was promised from the Manitoba and British Columbia Committee of the Baptist Convention of Ontario and Quebec, organized in 1888. Five thousand dollars a year for five years had been committed by Mr William Davies, founder of the meat packing empire that would become Canada Packers, and by other Davies family members. Further, the initial campaign in the Manitoba Convention had realized $14,510 in cash and pledges. After several false starts, a major Baptist venture in higher education in western Canada was on the brink of fulfilment.

The board of the new college met on 11 July 1899 to make the fateful decision on location. It approved a motion that "Brandon be selected as the home of the College for the present year."[15] However, before adjournment, the short term logic of amalgamation with Brandon Academy prevailed and the board decided to recommend to the Convention that the school's permanent location be in Brandon.

Brandon College opened 2 October 1899 in the Stewart Block with an enrolment of 110 and a faculty of seven. On 13 July 1900, amidst heady talk of formation of a Canada-wide Baptist Convention, delegates to the first National Baptist Convention, held in Winnipeg, boarded trains for Brandon to watch Mrs William Davies lay the cornerstone for Brandon Hall.

The location was a four-block site purchased from the city for three hundred dollars. It was south and west of the Assiniboine River on the outskirts of what Leland Clark describes as this "typical Western Canadian market centre-distribution depot" whose future would depend on its settled agricultural hinterland and its position as a divisional point for the developing railway grid.[16]

Meanwhile, discerning Baptists may have detected a subtle shift in educational priorities when the aim of the institution was described in the first Brandon College calendar. The design that emerged revealed that the agenda of eastern centrists had been exported to the west, for Brandon would have (1) an academy for young men, including programs leading to university matriculation, (2) training for young women equivalent to that of the most efficient ladies' colleges of Canada (thus a full music and expression department organized in 1907 was a prerequisite), (3) complete and thorough courses of business training, (4) a full university course in the department of arts, and (5) full theological courses.

In short, Brandon College was to be a prairie Woodstock, McMaster, and Moulton Hall all on a single campus. Further, the Christian philosophy of higher education was unequivocal. The *Annual Announcement* stated: "The College aims not only at the mental culture of its students but at the development of right character. It recognizes the supreme importance of surrounding the student during the period of college life with positive Christian influences, and to keep before him distinctively Christian ideals. The transcendent worth of character is kept in view in moulding the life of the College, while the best possible in intellectual training is sought."[17]

Obviously, no secular state institution could offer such an educational environment. On the other hand, churches bereft of pastors may well have questioned the requirement that preparatory work equivalent at least to the first two years' work of Manitoba University be required for entry to the theology department and wondered if the priorities of 1889 for Baptist higher education had not somehow been reversed.

Principal McDiarmid faced three major challenges during his twelve year tenure. The first, to gather a sound faculty, did not prove difficult. By 1910 the list included such names of subsequent eminence as Howard P. Whidden, future principal and McMaster Chancellor, noted economist Duncan A. MacGibbon, mathematician and physicist Arthur W. Vining, New Testament scholar Harris L. MacNeill, and classicist W. Sherwood Fox, future president of the University of Western Ontario, among others.

However, McDiarmid failed in the second challenge. He could not obtain from the recalcitrant Manitoba Legislature a charter amendment that would give Brandon College university status with the power to grant degrees. For Baptists, ideological and practical reasons demanded independence because the denomination did not believe in "the state dabbling in any ... sort of educational enterprise, except that which is initiated, supported and controlled by itself."[18] Practical circumstances added weight to the Baptist philosophy of separation of denominational education from state control. The curricular constraints dictated by the University of Manitoba were an infringement, and their examination procedures, which required students to write examinations in Winnipeg, were inefficient.

In consequence, the Baptists attempted in 1906 to gain a charter for "North Western University." McDiarmid appeared before the Private Bills Committee of the Manitoba Legislature in January 1907 and intimated that, if no charter were forthcoming, "affiliation with an Eastern University" was possible, and he held that the "monopoly principle" of the government could not be maintained. When it became clear that Brandon would not receive a charter amendment, and since Baptists were philosophically opposed to the monopoly principle and to association with denominational institutions that received public support, the school entered negotiations to affiliate with McMaster University. After hard bargaining, affiliation was achieved in April 1910 and the little McMaster on the prairies emerged, tied now to the same curricular constraints as they had experienced with the University of Manitoba and, as well, to eastern rigidities that would continue to inhibit response to the indigenous needs of the developing western frontier.[19]

Concurrently, debate over the vexatious question of priorities for denominational education remained. Some Baptists questioned the need for "an independent university," preferring to emphasize theological education and encourage other students to attend the fine state universities emerging in Saskatchewan, Alberta, and British Columbia. Such dissension occasioned McDiarmid's impassioned defence of Christian education before the Board of Governors in April 1907. He maintained, "our ideals differ from those of a state institution and therefore whatever the course our Provincial Institutions may take in the future, we ought to push for an independent university."[20]

Third, McDiarmid faced a widening gulf between the ambitions of the college and those of the emerging Baptist bureaucracy who were attempting to counter the anarchy of competing regional and special interests in the west. In 1907, the Baptists of British Columbia joined The Baptist Convention of Western Canada and finally, in 1909, the Baptist Union of Western Canada officially came into being. But some leaders expected these preliminary steps would culminate in a Baptist Union for Canada, then under active consideration of a Dominion-wide committee chaired by the Reverend H.F. Laflamme. They were disappointed. What did emerge in the west was a "Union" composed of four powerful competing provincial conventions, with often recalcitrant leadership ambitious for regional interests.

In 1909, the Reverend David B. Harkness was appointed successor to the Reverend W.T. Stackhouse as general secretary of the Baptist Union of Western Canada. Harkness was an enthusiastic centrist who had lobbied for a Baptist union for Canada and proposed a Baptist "University of Canada," composed of affiliated colleges in every region or province.[21] Hence, the constitution adopted by the Baptist Union of Western Canada in Moose Jaw on 11 November 1909 conflicted with the autonomous interests of Brandon College and Okanagan College, which was a sister academy founded in 1906 by British Columbia Baptists at Summerland on land donated by the Ritchie Bros., formerly from Rapid City. The constitution gave the Baptist Union "control of the home mission work, foreign mission work, publication and education work, carried on in the interests of the Baptists of Western Canada."[22]

The Education Board, composed of fourteen members elected by the Union, was soon challenged by provincial interests and educationalists who wished to pursue their own ambitious agendas independent of denominational control or priorities. For example, in the fall of 1909 the Brandon College Board planned a major financial appeal and deemed it "not wise" in view of the necessity for a "Forward Movement" — or financial campaign — that the "temporary arrangements made between the College Executive and the Home Mission Board be made permanent."[23] Two years later they openly challenged the "central policies relating to Forward Movements" and asserted that the "work of the College should be under the immediate and unfettered direction of its own Board of Directors and Senate."[24] It was a philosophic issue that would become a perennial problem in Baptist history in the west.

The outcome of this confrontation was the resignation on

4 September 1911 of McDiarmid who asserted that he had discovered that "some of the leaders of our denomination [were] not in sympathy with my ideals and policies for the development of Brandon College."[25] He maintained the issues were whether the full agenda for an academy, full arts college, ladies' college, and theological seminary would come to fruition.

Acrimonious debate attended the Baptist Union Assembly of January 1912 in Vancouver. The Education Board affirmed the status quo, counselling economic restraint. However, Professor Peter G. Mode, instructor in church history and practical theology at Brandon, broke ranks and advocated establishment of a theological seminary at Brandon in association with a provincial university and a liberal arts college further west. Already Alberta Baptists had procured the offer of land in Crescent Heights, Calgary, and a pledge of $25,000 from the widow of Mr A.J. McArthur, MLA for East Calgary, on condition that McArthur College came into being there.

Mode was supported by Reverend J.W. Litch and S.J. Farmer who represented the view that Baptists should maintain theological and academic (high school) work "while taking advantage of the provision made by the provinces for the teaching of Arts."[26]

Eventually a committee of seven was appointed by the assembly to consult with the provincial conventions on educational policy and report to the next annual meeting. However, the controversy left the denomination ill prepared to face the economic depression of 1913 which was to test the limited resources of its over extended constituency severely. McDiarmid retired to the Baptist community in Robman, British Columbia. Secretary Harkness resigned, frustrated, and eventually became general secretary of the Social Service Council of Manitoba. Mode returned to Brandon to be disciplined by the executive board, which, after voting for "permanent dismissal," eventually relented on condition he sign a letter of apology prepared by them. (So much for Baptist freedom of expression!) The Brandon College board even considered applying for an amendment of their charter so that the Board of Governors would be appointed by the Baptist Convention of Manitoba, rather than by the Baptist Union of Western Canada.[27]

The Brandon-Baptist Union controversy was a classic illustration of the kind of anarchy which resulted when educational interests and wider denominational objectives could not be resolved. Harris

MacNeill accused Baptist leaders of a conspiracy to destroy Brandon College. McDiarmid published correspondence from 1899 to establish that a commitment had been made to him for a full arts program. Peter Mode, now secure in the chair of church history at the University of Chicago, wrote to describe the educationalists' attitudes as "rivalry, *laissez-faire* survival of the fittest, among all the Baptist colleges that may choose to spring up in the West."[28] Even the astute W. Sherwood Fox addressed J.H. Farmer of McMaster to suggest that "Harkness to gain certain personal ends is trying to secure control of the college."[29]

In retrospect, one wonders that few denominationalists seemed to grasp the fact that all were fighting a rearguard action against the forces of secularization in higher education in Canada. For in a sense, Brandon College in 1899 was born out of step with the times, into a society that was moving rapidly to embrace state supported and controlled "secular" higher education.

On McDiarmid's departure the mantle of the presidency finally fell on Howard Primrose Whidden, BA, BTh, who had been professor of biblical literature and English at Brandon from 1900 to 1903, then minister of the affluent and "liberal" First Baptist Church of Dayton, Ohio. Born in 1871 in Antigonish of loyalist stock, he was a graduate of Acadia and McMaster, who, following a sojourn at the University of Chicago, had ministered in Morden, Manitoba, and Galt, Ontario, prior to joining the Brandon faculty in 1900. He accepted the presidency contingent on "assurances that the Arts department would be continued," an undertaking hardly iron clad in virtue of the mandate given the Education Board at the 1912 union Convention.[30]

The challenge was formidable. The "forces at work against Brandon College" had to be "conciliated," and her financial situation ameliorated.[31] For some years the college had been running financial deficits close to $10,000 per annum. Clark Hall, the women's residence opened in 1907, carried an outstanding mortgage of $30,000, and proceeds from the Forward Movement appeal, commenced in 1910 with a goal of $150,000 had raised only $41,000 in cash and $39,424 in pledges. Of the $128,000 in trust funds, $13,500 had been loaned internally for current needs and an estimated $50,000 was in Diamond Coal stock, shares of a doomed Baptist commercial enterprise near Drumheller, Alberta.

Dr C.W. Clark of Winnipeg, who was deeply involved in land

speculation, offered to assume the mortgage on Brandon College on condition "the Arts department [was] continued." Andrew Carnegie offered $25,000 provided that $60,000 in sustaining funds would be raised in eastern Canada and $15,000 from other sources. But terse word from the Rockefeller Foundation that their pledge to the Forward Movement of $50,000 was contingent on cash receipts of $100,000 and not on non-dividend bearing securities, proved a knock-out punch to the school in its desperate search for stability.[32]

Constraints prevent a detailed account of the impact of the 1913 depression which produced financial plight among the Baptist businessmen who supposedly had long been the college's mainstay. The first World War followed and inflation, coupled with decreased enrolment, added further complications. Suffice it to report that property held under the Clark Trust was heavily encumbered and the collapse of Diamond Coal sounded the *coup de grâce* to Okanagan College in 1915, and wiped out the paper assets of Brandon. By March 1917, Brandon's ledgers showed $107,000 in mortgages, bank loans, and current accounts outstanding.

The Brandon College Board responded with a decision that hindsight would rue. On a split vote of four to four, decided by the chair, and over the objections of J.P. Kilgour and Robert Darrach, it issued $100,000 in Brandon College bonds, with a twenty-year term to bear interest at 6 percent.[33] The American Baptist Publication Society took $30,000, the Imperial Bank of Canada $35,000 as collateral on loans, and the remainder was sold to sympathetic Baptists and Brandon residents.[34] This accomplished, Whidden was now freed to pursue his ambitions to expand the science faculty and strengthen the arts programs at the college.

While Whidden struggled with finances, western Baptists joined the holy crusade against the Kaiser. As at McMaster, the times demanded that classrooms be emptied for God and country. Lieutenants J.R.C. Evans and D.A. MacGibbon led the Canadian Officers Training Corps. In March 1916 the college platoon was organized and later joined the 196th Battalion, Western Universities, under Lieutenant W. Carey McKee, arriving in Britain in November 1916.[35] By the following spring, 280 students had enlisted, including two nursing sisters. Enrolment in the theology department was now five and there were only fifty-six in Arts. Total enrolment in 1917 was 230, down from 300 in 1916.

In February 1917, the Baptist Union set itself squarely behind the Borden administration's war policy, convinced that "only through a national non-partisan government, in which ... labour shall adequately be represented" could conscription be achieved and victory won.[36] Laurier's refusal to participate in a Union government divided pro-conscription from anti-conscription Liberals. Soon Brandon College became indirectly involved in the local expression of the national conflict.

First Brandon's Progressives, the Manitoba Grain Growers, and Labour Representation League met to choose a standard bearer for the impending election. The Reverend A.E. Smith, radical minister of First Methodist Church, later pastor of the Brandon Labour Church, had the support of organized labour. However, the nomination fell to Roderick McKenzie, secretary of the Manitoba Grain Growers. In the meantime, traditional unionists were deadlocked between Sir Augustus Nanton and T.A. Crerar of the United Grain Growers. The intervention of the Great War Veterans led to a convention that eventually nominated Howard P. Whidden over Roderick McKenzie. The disappointed "left" intended to nominate Brandon theology student Ernest S.L. Bisson, then on active service overseas, but were dissuaded when H.S. Paterson, a Winnipeg grain dealer was parachuted into the riding by Laurier Liberals. The election was never in doubt. Whidden was elected with 9,340 civilian votes as against 1,237 for Paterson and 2,125 military votes, while Paterson garnered only 92.[37]

Whether Brandon College and the Baptist Union prospered or suffered from their identification with the Union government is a question that merits further research. Certainly ethnic Baptists may well have remembered the discriminatory Wartime Elections Act of 1917 and the threats against Walter Rauschenbusch which resulted in the cancellation of his tour of western Canada when, in 1919, the North American Baptists severed their connections with the Baptist Union. And what role did member of Parliament Whidden play in the 1919 Civic Employees, Teamsters, and eventually, Brandon General, strikes? Did his support of the Bordon administration have a detrimental effect on Brandon's working class and ethnic communities and influence their ballots when financial assistance was solicited for Brandon College in future years?[38]

In 1920, historian Chester W. New moved to McMaster University.

Oral tradition in Brandon credits him with outspoken sympathy for labour in the 1919 strikes. Did possible differences with Whidden influence his move? Finally, to what degree were students and faculty involved with Salem Bland's colourful supporter, the Reverend A.E. Smith and the People's Church of Brandon as an expression of the social gospel inclinations of the school?

Answers to such intriguing questions as these are essential if we are to address critically the question of whether "those good old Baptist social gospellers that we [have] come to know and love"[39] were really active practitioners of progressive social Christianity, or merely persons of liberal temperament who accepted moderate biblical criticism, and embraced the moral and intellectual currents of the period.

With the advent of the 1920s, economic prosperity slowly returned to the west. In Whidden's view, the time was now ripe for the college to meet the "increased demand" for work in junior college science. A worthy science building was required. It was provided eventually through funds subscribed primarily by the citizens of Brandon; a fact not lost on Whidden when he negotiated with Hamilton civic officials for McMaster's removal there from Toronto in 1930. However, the increase in capital debt of $30,000 and added current expenses for science faculty in the face of the de facto loss of the theological department did little to endear the college to agrarian and blue collar Baptists in the west.

Concurrently, the will of Brandon's first benefactor, William Davies, included a bequest for $100,000, provided friends would provide a similar amount. This was accomplished through careful management and extended effort among a modest constituency. But Brandon's resources remained precarious, while the expansion of her curriculum continued in areas determined more by academic interests and faculty pressure than constituency consensus.

Meanwhile, Brandon College and the Baptist Union were about to be convulsed by a major skirmish related to the fundamentalist-modernist controversy. Associated as the college was with McMaster for curriculum and "mainline" American Baptist institutions for faculty, the school reflected the *zeitgeist* of moderate theological thought and rhetorical social Christianity. Hence it was not immune to theological conflicts originating elsewhere.

In 1909, Dr Elmore Harris of Walmer Road Baptist Church, Toronto had accused Professor I.G. Matthews of McMaster of liberalism, charges dismissed by the Baptist Convention of Ontario and Quebec. But at the time Brandon's McDiarmid commented that had Harris been successful in putting McMaster "out of business" he would have turned his guns "on the heretics of Brandon."[40]

Nevertheless, this did not deter the school from associating with "mainline" Baptists from the University of Chicago, Crozer, and Rochester. For example, in 1913 Brandon's Commencement speaker was Dr George Cross, the christocentric theologian who preached that "religion that sees Christ interprets God in terms of Christ's nature." "Such a faith," he asserted, "is not subject to forms and cannot have any fixed form of doctrine."[41] It was, indeed, a challenge to Baptist confessionalists.

Whidden had studied at Chicago, and three decades earlier had written that while it was not exactly a hotbed of heresy, pretty tall heretics grew there from time to time.[42] Yet he seems to have been sincerely unprepared when charges of modernism were made by a former Brandon student, John Linton, and the Vancouver Baptist ministerial related to the theology of Professors Carl H. Lager and Harris Lachlan MacNeill of Brandon College.

The Brandon College Commission set up by the Baptist Union found Lager orthodox but his relations with the Swedish Conference strained. MacNeill's frank uncertainty on such issues as the virgin birth, the penal substitutionary theory of the atonement, and eschatology fueled regional unrest and eventually led in 1927 to the founding of the schismatic Convention of Regular Baptists of British Columbia.[43] The sustained theological controversy throughout the 1920s increased the apathy among Baptists towards an institution whose goals no longer included a primary emphasis on the training of leadership for the churches. Amidst such turmoil, in 1923 Whidden resigned to become chancellor of McMaster University.

Clearly, Whidden and his associates did not appreciate the level of discontent and resolute resolve of Baptist democrats, nor the impact the fundamentalist-modernist controversies would have on Baptist higher education. This is confirmed by the fact that immediately upon arriving in Toronto, and after recommending President Burton of Chicago, McMaster bestowed an honorary doctorate on Dr W.H.P. Faunce, the redoubtable exponent of liberal higher education independent of control by the masses. Faunce was then president of Brown University. Dr T.T. Shields, a disciple of Spurgeon, needed little more ammunition than "the condition of affairs in the West" under the presidency of Dr Whidden to conclude that "to aid and abet the destructive work of Brandon College was nothing short of treason to Christ and His gospel."[44]

Whidden left federal politics in 1921 and was installed as chancellor of McMaster University in November 1923. His departure left Brandon bereft of a president and a much needed practical theologian. The 1923 report of the Commission of Inquiry had registered the unrest of Baptists with the fact that, since 1917, theological and arts work had been combined and the degree program for clergy discontinued.

In March of that year the board offered the professorship in practical theology to the Reverend M.F. McCutcheon of Montreal, who declined. On 21 May they offered the presidency and faculty position to Dr Franklin W. Sweet, minister of the Church of the Master, Cleveland, Ohio. Sweet was a graduate of Denison University (1889) and Rochester Seminary (1893). He had conducted a crusade at Brandon in 1913, received an honorary DD from Des Moines University (1917), and had been pastor of Calvary Baptist Church, Minneapolis, before he accepted the pulpit of a church dominated by Canadian expatriates in Cleveland.

Further, since 1920, Sweet had served as secretary of the Committee of Nine appointed by the Northern Baptist Convention of the United States to "inquire into the loyalty of our Baptist schools to Jesus Christ and his Gospel."[45] His conciliatory reputation was to prove invaluable at the enlarged Baptist Union Assembly, held in Calgary in January 1924, when the religious teaching of Brandon came under review.[46]

During his brief administration, which concluded with his sudden death in December 1924, Sweet supported the policy that "Arts work should be our first consideration," and he appears to have had little success in modifying the religion courses as recommended by the commission to provide for Bible survey instead of a literary critical approach. Perhaps this was because curriculum content was determined by the "mother house" at McMaster. But Sweet did welcome expatriate Canadian, Dr J.W.A. Stewart, former dean of Rochester Seminary to strengthen the religion program.[47] That same year the board approved use of funds set aside to build the College Memorial Gymnasium to cover pressing current expenses.

Upon Sweet's death, Dean Harris MacNeill was appointed to carry the administrative responsibilities of president while the board, chaired by the able Brandon Baptist, Robert Darrach, searched for a successor. The position was offered first to the Reverend John McLaurin, who declined. Finally the lot fell to the Reverend David Bovington, DD, minister of the First Baptist Church of Cleveland. An Englishman, Bovington first attended Spurgeon's College, then Woodstock, and graduated from McMaster in 1899. After pastorates in Windsor and St. Thomas he became instructor in systematic theology at Rochester under the orthodox Charles A. Strong prior to his nine year tenure in Cleveland.

Arriving in midsummer 1925, Bovington served notice that he intended to strengthen "theological courses," encourage the tutorial Dalton plan in the academy, set up a special committee to revise the "values placed on certain assets," and renew the struggle to secure a university charter from the provincial government.[48] Enrolment was encouraging. That year there were 349 students, of whom 204 were in arts and theology. On the other hand, the fundamentalist-modernist controversy in the Union continued unabated. Brandon also faced a major financial crisis, because the Davies Foundation grants — which amounted to 23 per cent of the current income — concluded that year. In addition, tension between McMaster and the Brandon Senate resurfaced as the school struggled with the "need and opportunity of making suitable adaptations to a western and particularly rural constituency."[49]

Internal dissension surfaced in June 1926 when Old Testament Professor C.H. Lager complained that for six years there had been no dean of theology, and the work which "was supremely in the minds of the founders of Brandon College" and Baptists remained without leadership. He warned that the "promising 23" would "switch into arts and become public or hi school teachers, but not ministers or missionaries."[50]

The Reverend H.H. Bingham of Calgary spoke for many western Baptists when he expressed to Chancellor Whidden of McMaster his deep concern for the future of Brandon. In his view, the college was "getting further and further from the hearts of the denomination in the West." "It [was] more and more in the hands of a few who might be termed local men," he concluded. Funding for undergraduate education was lost when students went "to the other side" (the United States), the very thing Brandon had been founded to prevent.[51]

Overwhelmed, Bovington, after six months, had already submitted his resignation. In his letter of resignation he wrote, "I came with little or no knowledge of your problems. They proved more difficult than I anticipated ... I hope my action may not be interpreted as an attempt to escape tasks and difficulties which I have assumed, but rather readiness to permit you to plan freely for the pressing problems with which you are confronted."[52]

For two more years Dr Harris MacNeill struggled on as acting president. The theological controversy made him an unacceptable successor to Bovington. Finally, in April 1928, he resigned after twenty-seven years at Brandon to become minister of Fairview Baptist Church, Vancouver. The "local men" that September offered the presidency to long time faculty member Dr J.R.C. Evans. Evans was a graduate of the academy and of the college (1907), trained in mathematics and science. On leave of absence from 1920-3, he had received his doctorate in geology from the University of Chicago. Since he had lived the Brandon story, the board reasoned he might be able to accomplish what wise "clergymen" from the east had failed to do.

Again the Baptist Union set up a committee to investigate theological training and examine the financial crises at Brandon. In 1928 they recommended that, subject to finances, the arts department be maintained but not expanded, that a department of religion be formed to grant a BTh to students taking less than a full arts program, and that the academy and music departments bear their "own costs through fees charged." In the early '20s the school had opted for independence of the Union budget and instead made direct appeals to patrons and churches. Now the denominational obligation was stressed and the Union loaned Brandon a second $10,000 to assist with the annual current deficit, estimated at $45,000.[53]

In the spring of 1929, Brandon College launched a financial drive that appeared impressive. However, as in the past, it was an all or nothing carrot offered on a conditional basis by wealthy philanthropists. *The Western Baptist* announced that Cyrus Eaton of Cleveland, G.C. Edwards of Ottawa, and A.E. McKenzie of Brandon, had subscribed $750,000 on the following terms:

[O]f this $750,000 subscribed, $550,000 is immediately interest-bearing, that is to say, the immediate maintenance of the College will be assisted through quarterly gifts amounting to interest at 5 1/2 percent of $550,000. Interest payments will be made quarterly up until June 1st next year, at which time they will automatically cease unless friends of the College in Western Canada have met the first condition of the endowment gift. In order to meet this condition, the College is undertaking a campaign to raise $150,000 by June 1st, 1930 ... If this condition is met the principal donors agree to continue their quarterly interest payments until December 31st, 1933, by which time the College must raise a total sum of $500,000 in cash. Upon the fulfilment of this second condition the capital sum of three quarters of a million dollars will be legally payable to Brandon College, which will hereafter receive the interest earned by the endowment.[54]

The financial appeal program was a gargantuan challenge in the best of times for a denomination with an annual budget of $300,000. It was a pious hope under the circumstances. The Wall Street crash of August 1929 coincided with the campaign. The fundamentalist-modernist schism left a weakened constituency. In the east, the transfer of McMaster, the voracious matron of Bloor Street to Hamilton demanded the full resources of Baptist philanthropists.

By July 1930, only $40,000 in cash had been received. In January 1931, the board of the Baptist Union met in Edmonton and reluctantly resolved that "the Board of Brandon College be requested ... in view of the inability of the Baptist Union to make provision for adequate financial support, the College cease to operate at the end of the current College year and that the Brandon College Board wind up the affairs of the College in such manner as to it may deem wise."[55]

Who controlled the college became the immediate issue, because the president and localities on the Brandon College Board with many on the faculty did not deem closure "wise." As Professor S.J. McKee expressed it, "no denominational board had a right to make such a momentous decision."[56] The Brandon College Board did not take seriously the Union directive, but responded by abandoning the Baptist principle of separation of church and state to lobby the Manitoba government for assistance. When that failed, they persuaded the City of Brandon to submit a bylaw to ratepayers that would have authorized a tax levy of $20,000 a year for five years on behalf of the school.

The measure failed when it received 58 percent of the vote, short of the 60 percent required for approval. The defeat was attributable to the north wards, inhabited by ethnic minorities and railway and blue collar workers, for whom the school provided no personal or business benefit. In response, a citizen's college campaign was launched, which raised $20,000. On the basis of this temporary respite, the school reopened.

The decade of the 1930s witnesses heroic efforts to maintain Brandon College amidst the problems created by drought and depression. Whereas, in 1929, Baptist Union mission receipts from the three prairie provinces were $340,000, the figure fell to $173,000 by 1938. Brandon financial appeals were similarly affected when the various honour campaigns consistently fell short of their goals as deficits mounted. In 1930, the college defaulted on interest payments to bond holders. In 1932 the "retired" Professor C.H. Lager only refrained from taking court action for "bankruptcy" when his bonds were redeemed through an ingenious arrangement between the board and Mr Robert Darrach.[57]

In the meantime, the "retreat of the Union Baptists from small villages was no less significant." Sociologist William E. Mann reports that "over 80 of the prairie churches were closed between 1914 and 1944."[58] Actually, the number remained almost static between 1928 (when there were 127) and 1938 (when the number was 122). However, in British Columbia, the figure declined from 48 in 1926 to 29 in 1938, primarily as a result of the fundamentalist-modernist schism.

Brandon College responded to the great depression by closing the academy and business departments in 1932. Both were victims of decreased enrolment and the expansion of secular secondary and technical education elsewhere. Sporadic attempts were made to maintain a department of religion when Dr C.B. Lumsden was appointed to the faculty in 1935, and Reverend E.M. Whidden the following year. Heroic sacrifices were made by the faculty and staff, as is illustrated by the fact that, by 1938, $36,000 of the $49,000 in current deficits were salaries outstanding.

Eventually, in June 1937, the Baptist Union dusted off the proposal of 1912 that a separate theological school be founded elsewhere and that students take arts training in state universities. But finally, in November of that year, the Union board reluctantly resolved that "unless additional financial support can be obtained ... the Union Board ... recommend to the Union at the next meeting that the College be closed."[59] A disbelieving President Evans assured his executive committee that this was the same resolution as one defeated by the assembly in June and that "Mr Smalley [executive secretary and Brandon alumnus] phoned me from Saskatoon on November 22nd, asking that no notice be taken of it."[60]

However, facts were facts. Under depression conditions, the college deficits placed the whole Baptist Union enterprise in jeopardy. The Union board remained resolute. Appeal to the annual assembly was to no avail and a more strongly worded resolution than that of 1931 was approved which stated, "... the Baptist Union of Western Canada authorizes and requests the Brandon College Board to endeavour to make any arrangement for the continuing on of the college work which the said Board may deem wise, even if this should entail amendment of the Act of incorporation in such a way as to, in effect, mean the giving of the College to those prepared to carry it on."[61]

Throughout the spring of 1938, pressure was exerted to obtain financial assistance to sustain a non-sectarian Brandon from the financially hard pressed provincial government of the Honourable John Bracken. First, a committee struck by the Brandon Chamber of Commerce requested the government to provide $30,000 a year for twenty years. Later, a delegation representing twenty-nine communities in western Manitoba lobbied both the Honourable Ivan Schultz, the minister of education, and the premier. It was to no avail.

Paradoxically, the savior of Brandon College turned out to be the local seed merchant and board member, Mr A.E. McKenzie. When the financial campaign of 1930 ended in failure, he wrote to Dr Evans, "If the College is to be saved permanently, only Brandon men can and will save it."[62] On 13 July 1938, through the good offices of Mr Isaac Pitblado, KC, he did. He offered to set up an endowment of $300,000, provided the provincial government would guarantee an annual grant of $35,000 a year for twenty years. Subsequent negotiations increased the endowment to $500,000, with the provincial government providing $22,500 a year and the ratepayers of Brandon $5,000 per annum. Legislation followed which granted Brandon College the status of an affiliate of the University of Manitoba.

On 31 August 1938, Brandon College passed from Baptist hands and became the responsibility of a provisional board. It remained for the previous board through the Baptist Union to discharge an estimated $25,000 in current liabilities to teachers, staff, and local tradesmen. Finally, on 25 October 1938, the Baptists severed their legal connections and ended a forty year excursion into the field of higher education.[63]

In *The Modern Schism*, the noted historian Martin Marty suggests that as early as the mid-Victorian period the purposes and goals of higher education in North America were changing, that training for the ministry was giving way to secular concerns, to a rapid declericalization of education, and to specialization. The very cost of higher education forced it from the church into the hands of the state, as foreign university models supplanted the evangelical seminary concept.[64]

On the one hand, in the history of Brandon College we find an institution struggling with secularization, seeking with limited resources to provide Christian higher education, confused with its loyalty towards the Baptist denomination and those who would have it evolve into a stellar regional college.

Concurrently, one finds the undermining by class and professionalism of the communitarian values cherished by so many Baptist democrats. Higher education was and is an inherently elite enterprise. Keeping pace with the times for eastern oriented leaders meant building a university to rival McGill or McMaster. Keeping pace with the times for rural and working class Baptists meant having a pastor, "Arts or no arts, theology or no theology."

McMaster historian Charles M. Johnston suggests that blue collar Baptists may have found it difficult to share the deepest feelings of leaders like Howard Primrose Whidden, the well-placed professional who moved so "affably among the affluent Baptists of Manitoba and [the] prosperous citizens of Dayton."[65] Well they might have asked themselves if it was not possible (to turn a phrase famous in Baptist history) that on occasion Brandon College imagined that the denomination existed for Brandon, not Brandon for the denomination?[66]

This was no expression of anti-intellectualism. It was born from frank recognition of the kind of education to which blue collar Baptists could realistically aspire. In the 1890s, Moody Institute,

Chicago, and Toronto Bible College pioneered an educational model that offered biblical training often in tandem with secondary or academy courses. The bible school movement arrived in western Canada in 1922 and burgeoned as mainline denominational seminaries and colleges declined. By 1947, there were 24 sectarian, and 8 non-sectarian bible colleges in the west which provided populist functional education in a Christian environment at realistic cost.[67]

The history of Brandon College also illustrates the secularization of private philanthropy in North America. The Victorian age was one where colleges and seminaries reaped "a harvest from the acquisitive, exploitive middle-class."[68] Financial independence freed them from denominational control. Ontario Baptists had Senator William McMaster. However, apart from his rival, William Davies, no major benefactor appeared for Okanagan or Brandon College, and there was no sustaining endowment. At the same time, as early as the founding of the University of Chicago in 1893, John D. Rockefeller and his contemporaries began to signal their move away from support of denominational enterprises when they turned their attention to ecumenical and secular alternatives.

The impression prevails that Brandon College, like McMaster, depended on the munificence of wealthy benefactors. In reality, it depended on incentives from benefactors (seldom realized), on the sacrifice of ordinary Baptists and Brandon citizens, on a dedicated faculty, ingenious and sometimes questionable financial manipulation, on tenacious hope, and "tomorrow country" optimism.

Sub-themes from the Brandon College story include the issue of provincial rivalries among Baptists, as it related to education. Many were the vexatious difficulties posed as congregationalists struggled to devise a polity appropriate to the twentieth century. Brandon's ambivalent relationship to McMaster merits further study as the school attempted to adjust to the needs of the indigenous west fettered by academic rigidities and agendas set elsewhere. For academics, tension developed as they were forced to relate to conflicting aims and values posed by their Christian commitment, and the demands of an increasingly secular world community of scholars.

A truth that contemporary Baptist Union leaders may discover is the fact that ownership of education must ultimately come from the "heart sweat" of the people. Indigenous location does not and did not automatically guarantee functional education or indigenous identification. Affluent Baptists followed their agenda while churches, bereft of clergy, adopted populist alternatives. It was Peter Mode who warned against trying to reproduce ivy-covered institutions on the frontier.[69]

On the other hand, any assessment of the history of Brandon College would be remiss if it were made solely on the basis of sociological, educational, or institutional criteria. Our Baptist ancestors were supremely convinced that education must issue in "the development of right character," and they believed that this could be achieved by "surrounding the student during the period of college life with positive Christian influences and ideals." It was an inherently liberal commitment.

On the basis of this criteria, Brandon College was an unqualified success because her legacy was and is in her graduates. In public life alone we can point to the Honourable John Bowen, first graduate in theology and lieutenant governor of Alberta. There is T.C. Douglas, premier of Saskatchewan and first leader of the New Democratic Party, there is Premier Douglas Campbell of Manitoba, not to mention the conscience of the House of Commons, the Honourable Stanley Knowles. Olive Freeman Diefenbaker and Beatrice Brigdon likewise served their generation from widely different political perspectives. Similarly, in the fields of religion, education, science, and business the list of distinguished alumni is impressive.

Brandon University stands today above the banks of the Assiniboine as the proud successor of Brandon College. It is a regional university with a student body of 3,100. In 1966, the province of Manitoba, which through the decades insisted on a monopoly for the University of Manitoba, passed the Universities Establishment Act. Under Order-in-Council 50 (1967), Brandon University was established as an independent degree granting institution. (Sixty years later Dr A.P. McDiarmid obtained his precious charter amendment).

We leave the final word to Dr Watson Kirkconnell, the Baptist statesman of higher education. He witnessed the passing of a generation of dedicated Christian scholars, and wrote for our benefit:

Though we speak with tongues of learning
We are but as sounding brass
If mere knowledge, undiscerning
Darkly view Thee through a glass.
God of Heaven, teach us ever
Love, that doth all loves surpass.[70]

J . R . C .   P E R K I N

"There Were Giants in The Earth in Those Days" : An Assessment of Watson Kirkconnell

In the early hours of 16 July 1925, two young men were sleeping fitfully just inside the main door of the Ross Memorial Hospital, in Lindsay, Ontario. The hospital staff had thoughtfully provided two small cots so that the men could rest, but their anxiety was such that proper sleep was impossible. One of them was a professor of English from Wesley College, Winnipeg; he had returned to his native region for a holiday. At about noon on the previous day his wife, the former Isabel Peel, had given birth to twin boys. The babies were fairly healthy, but she had gradually weakened during the afternoon and by evening was critically ill. The other young man was a friend of the professor and a son of the physician who was battling to save the young mother's life.

At about 4 a.m., the young men were suddenly brought to full consciousness by a loud knocking on the door, only a few feet from where they lay. They leaped up and rushed to the door, eager to help in whatever emergency situation had arisen. But when they opened the door, there was no one there and no sound except that of the torrential summer rain beating on the ground.

The two men stood in shocked silence and then heard footsteps behind them. They turned to see a nurse who beckoned to the husband. He hurried with her to the bedside of his wife, who died within a few minutes of his arrival.[1]

The young professor was Watson Kirkconnell, born on 16 May 1895 to Thomas Kirkconnell, who at the time was headmaster of the local high school, and his wife, the former Bertha Watson. In 1908, Thomas was appointed principal of the Lindsay Collegiate Institute, and it was here that Watson obtained his high school education, which culminated in July 1913 with successful completion of no less than seventeen senior matriculation examination papers. In the fall of the same year, Watson entered the honours classics program at Queen's University. He received his MA in 1916 and won the medal for both Latin and Greek.

After a short time on the staff of the Royal Military College in Kingston, Kirkconnell was transferred to the 253rd Battalion, Canadian Expeditionary Force, expecting to go overseas. However, he was found to be medically unfit for overseas duty and spent the next three years as a captain with the Department of Internment Operations. At the end of the war, Kirkconnell was in Britain, responsible for the transport of several hundred German prisoners of war who were being repatriated. He returned to Canada too late for admission to any graduate program and unable to follow a secondary intention of training as a professional singer due to a life-long susceptibility to laryngitis. For a time Kirkconnell toyed with the idea of a career in journalism, even completing a correspondence course, but in 1921 the Imperial Order of the Daughters of the Empire chose him as their first overseas scholar for Ontario. He spent the academic year 1921-2 in Oxford, studying for the B.Litt degree and enjoying the opportunity to visit Europe, cycle around the Oxfordshire countryside, and enter fully into the life of Lincoln College and the university.

Late in the summer of 1922, Kirkconnell was preparing his B.Litt thesis, *"International Aspects of Unemployment,"* for publication when he was invited to fill a short-term vacancy at Wesley College. The one year appointment resulted in an eighteen year stay, eleven years in the Department of English and the remainder as head of the Department of Classics. In 1924, he married Isabel Peel; the couple had returned to Lindsay in 1925 so that the babies could be born there.[2]

The loss of his wife shattered several aspects of the life Kirkconnell had been building since joining the faculty of Wesley College. It destroyed the almost idyllic home life he had enjoyed with Isabel Peel for one short year; it constituted the first serious test of the Christian faith he had hitherto accepted as a part of his thinking and outlook; and it drove him to seek occupation for his mind and solace for his spirit in one of the most ambitious literary projects ever attempted by an individual. He decided, as a memorial to his wife, to translate into English verse all the elegies he could find in European languages, both ancient and modern. Forty years later he was to describe the project thus: "Books were secured from all over Europe, and through winter nights that might otherwise have seemed interminable, I poured my grief and my linguistic zeal into the task."[3]

Incredible as it may seem, by April 1926 the work was almost complete and a manuscript containing translations of elegies from no less than forty languages as different as Latin, German, Portuguese, Polish, Welsh, Finnish, and Icelandic was ready for the press of some adventurous publisher.

The collection contained "Clouds of Silver", translated from Finnish:

> Clouds of silver, clouds of silver
> Ride and race and soar
> On beyond the blue horizon
> And return no more.
>
> Fair they flash and gleam and glitter,
> Laughing in the light,
> And behind far golden portals
> Vanish from the sight.
>
> So bright days of perfect pleasure
> Pass and disappear,
> Leaving the cold hail of sorrow
> To its task austere.[4]

Kirkconnell's rendering of a Romany folksong from Hungary was entitled "Mourning":

> Everywhere I pass to-day
> Cold rocks wall my wretched way;
> Down the granite wastes a-wing,
> Winter winds have slain the spring,

As my frosts of grief have done,
Marring May when scarce begun,
Nor can showers of my weeping
Rouse that dead joy from its sleeping.
Could I be the grave's dark guest,
I would gladly take my rest.[5]

It is not hard to understand why Kirkconnell chose these elegies; they spoke to his sense of loneliness and anguish that so spring-like a romance had succumbed so soon to the deadly winter frosts of mortality. The last poem in the collection, translated from the Swedish and called "A Man's Last Word to a Woman," summarizes Kirkconnell's grief in a mere six lines:

I followed, flushed with hope, thy path of roses
In springtime's radiant dawn and showery stress;

The record of our summer love discloses
Noontides of passion past all power of guess;

And in the autumn gloom, when the act closes,
I give thee thanks, who wert my happiness.[6]

Despite the industry and achievement apparent in the poetry, serious obstacles were in the path of its publication. On 3 April 1926, Kirkconnell wrote to Messrs George Allen & Unwin, the British firm which had published *International Aspects of Unemployment*, offering them the translations under the title "A European Book of Elegy," subtitled "a collection of 100 poems, predominantly elegiac in tone, chosen and translated by myself from some forty different languages, past and present." The letter included the statements:

So far as I am aware, no work of translation on so catholic a scale has ever been attempted in any country. The nature of the selections, too, is such that the work might appeal to the general public as well as to the scholar ...

... I should be grateful if you would, in stating your attitude towards such a volume, give me at the same time your candid advice on one point. Would you think it desirable to print throughout, on opposite pages to the translations, the original of the forty languages? [7]

Reflecting on this letter almost forty years later, Kirkconnell would see it in perspective and was able to write: "Such a letter from a man known to them only as the author ... of a successful volume in Economics, apparently gave Allen & Unwin justifiable doubts as to my sanity."[8]

Certainly, the response was unequivocal. The managing editor of the press, a Mr Skinner, replied on 14 April 1926 as follows:

Dear Sir,
We thank you for your letter of April 3rd and enclosures. While we shall be very willing to consider the complete MS of your "European Book of Elegy" when ready, we very much doubt whether we shall see our way to make a proposal for its publication.
As you ask for our "candid advice", we will say quite frankly that we think you have undertaken too big a task. We do not believe there is any living man so intimately acquainted with forty different European languages, past and present, as to be able to translate poems from those languages.

Yours faithfully,[9]

Kirkconnell was still emotionally vulnerable from his bereavement and intellectually exhausted from the phenomenal labours of the previous months. Whereas other people, in similar circumstances, might have given up the publication project, he became more determined to carry it through. It was as though his grief required that his translations appear in print and his intellectual integrity required that the accuracy of his work be certified by scholars of unquestioned reputation. So he sent copies of selections of the original poems and the translations to the scholars most likely to be able to determine the quality of his work. For example, the poems translated from Slavonic languages were sent to Professor Nevill Forbes of Oxford University and the translations from Romance languages were sent to Professor Raymond Weeks of Columbia University. Without exception the responses were positive.

Professor Forbes expressed his views on the difficulty of the project Kirkconnell had undertaken as follows: "As regards the actual translations, I hold very pronounced views on the rendering of rhymed poems in any Slavonic language into rhymed English verse. Briefly, I consider it is virtually impossible to do that & at the same time reproduce the CONTENT of the Slavonic poem."

Despite these misgivings, Forbes' concluding paragraph included the comment: "On the whole your work seems to me highly success- ful & I am sure you need have no doubts but that it is 'a worthy memorial'."[10]

Professor Weeks' comments began with the words: "I am your debtor for the pleasure with which I have read this collection of brilliant translations from the Latin and Romance languages." Forbes made several technical points, along with a suggestion to include another poem.[11]

Despite this recognition, much work remained to be done; the copyright for each poem had to be obtained and a publisher found who was willing to take the commercial risk involved in printing such a volume. Eventually The Graphic Publishers of Ottawa, a firm which prided itself on the production of "Canadian Books of Con- sequence" agreed to print the translations (although not the original poems), along with brief notes on the poets and an introductory essay on verse translation. In 1928, the volume appeared with the title *European Elegies: 100 Poems Chosen and Translated from European Literatures in 50 languages*. It was a book of 166 pages, clearly printed and well bound.

The poems were grouped into five sections — Autumn, Winter, Spring, Summer, Autumn — with Verner von Heidenstam's poem "A Man's Last Word to a Woman" standing alone at the end. There was an extended introduction, dealing with the whole question of verse translation,[12] and brief biographical notes on the poets.

Critical response to *European Elegies* was swift and positive. The Kirkconnell papers include scores of letters, written in dozens of languages, expressing appreciation of the beauty of the translations and incredulity at the linguistic achievement they represent. One point frequently made was that the poems do not read at all like translations, but might stand as poetic creations in their own right. Several academics referred appreciatively to the introduction. Ray- mond Weeks, whose reaction to the manuscript had been cautious, was delighted with the translations and particularly complimentary concerning the introduction.[13] Quotations from two reviews will serve to illustrate the public and professional response to the publica- tion. *The Montreal Star* on 18 August 1928 began its review thus: "No more remarkable book than Professor Watson Kirkconnell's *European Elegies* (The Graphic Publishers) has ever appeared in Canada."

An Icelandic review, published in Reykjavik, included the comment: "One thing is certain, since Tennyson achieved IN MEMORIAM, this book is the most glorious wreath that any man has laid at the grave of the beloved dead."

Such a fascinating story surely ought to conclude with a comment that the book established Kirkconnell's fame and fortune. It certainly established his fame, and the literary world was aware that there was a new star in the linguistic firmament, but there was no fortune. The Graphic Publishers subsequently went bankrupt and the accountant responsible for winding up their estate wrote to Kirkconnell, acknowledging that he should have received a royalty cheque for $744.00, but enclosing a proportional payment in the form of a cheque for $2.05!

This story has been told at some length because I believe that it is the clue to an understanding of what I suggest is Kirkconnell's single most important contribution to Canadian society and higher education. A project which began as a solace for personal grief introduced him to the elegiac literature of many nations. Immigrants from several of these nations had come to Canada and had settled on the prairies in the late nineteenth and early twentieth centuries, with a major influx immediately following the First World War. These immigrants had tended to stay in national groups, so that the Ukrainians would settle in one area, the Hungarians in another, and so on. Once the battle for simple survival was over, churches were built and conscious efforts were made to maintain ethnic heritages by educational, religious, and cultural societies. Newspapers began to appear, keeping alive the languages, publishing articles and poems, providing valuable information for farmers and families, and giving a sense of identity to the local communities. Almost alone among the Canadians of his day, Kirkconnell was able to become both an observer of, and a participant in, this process.[14]

Inevitably, Kirkconnell's interest in the immigrant literature brought him into contact with the authors and their families. In later years, when the children of some immigrants sought admission to universities, it was to Kirkconnell that parents turned for information and advice and his counsel invariably had a double motivation — to enable the young people to achieve their full potential, thus contributing as much as possible to Canadian society, and to encourage them to know and respect the ethnic inheritance that was theirs.[15]

Kirkconnell was one of the few scholars in the Canada of the 1920s and 1930s who seemed able to enter into the yearnings and frustrations of immigrant groups, to read and understand their literature, whether written in their homeland or their new country, and to recognize the role that these peoples might play in the development of Canadian culture and identity. He saw for them not merely equality before the law or even equality of opportunity, but an acceptance based on the recognition that their contribution was essential to the emergence of true Canadian nationhood and political identity. In this sense, I believe that Kirkconnell may be described as one of the fathers of Canadian multiculturalism, in the broadest and richest meaning of that term. This, I would claim, was his first and most important contribution to Canadian society and higher education.[16]

It is at this point that I believe we see the influence of the Baptist upbringing which shaped much of Kirkconnell's thinking about what today we would call human rights and equality of opportunity. He had been brought up in what one might regard as a classical Baptist tradition, characterized by a high regard for education, a love of personal freedom, and a readiness to defend the rights of others — particularly those who were part of a disadvantaged group. These attitudes, blended with his insatiable intellectual curiosity and enormous capacity for sustained industry, partially explain Kirkconnell's concern for immigrant people and his ability to express that concern in practical and effective ways. In short, it was his blend of emotional experience, intellectual capacity, and spiritual inheritance that led him to attempt and achieve objectives which justify our speaking of him as the father of Canadian multiculturalism.

In 1934, the Canadian Polish Society was formed in Winnipeg and Kirkconnell became its first president, the first of many similar offices he was to hold. In 1938, he and Hope (whom he had married in 1930) visited Hungary where Watson lectured at the summer school in the University of Debrecen.[17] Such contacts as this increased his awareness of the culture which had been brought to Canada by the immigrants and made him the more determined that it should not be lost.

Throughout his eighteen years in Winnipeg, Kirkconnell was constantly building up his library of dictionaries and grammars and tracked down and registered in his files the names of authors and poets who wrote in the immigrant languages, as well as noting and collecting copies of the scores of ethnic magazines, newspapers, and journals which had been published, many of them lasting only a short time. Due to his industry, this information was secured and documented; but for him much of the early material would have disappeared without trace.

One result of Kirkconnell's interest and industry in relation to immigrant poets was the publication in 1935 of *Canadian Overtones*, a little book of just over 100 pages with a descriptive subtitle: "An Anthology of Canadian Poetry written originally in Icelandic, Swedish, Norwegian, Hungarian, Italian, Greek, and Ukrainian, and now translated and edited with biographical, historical, critical, and bibliographical notes." The preface begins: "This book seeks to reveal to English-speaking Canadians a transient but intensely significant phase of our national literature." Forty-three different poets are represented and they describe the whole range of immigrant life. Sigurbjorn Johannsson (1839-1903) came to Canada from Iceland in 1889 and encountered extreme hardship, reflected in his brief poem "Emigration to Canada."

> I never knew what Dearth's grim hand
> To starving mortals meant
> Until from out my native land
> It gave me banishment.
>
> With half my lifetime thrown away,
> In exile I must toil,
> And rest, when ends my human day,
> In this cold alien soil.[18]

By contrast, Sten Wiktor Goerwell, who came to Canada from Sweden in 1920, was optimistic about his future. Soon after his arrival he wrote a four stanza poem entitled "Fifteen Cents in My Pocket"; the last verse runs:

> Fifteen Cents in My Pocket,
> Merriment in my heart,
> A loving maid in remembrance —
> Grief is a world apart.

Soon shall the joys of Yuletide
Echo the wide world through;
Soon shall the peace of Christmas
Sit at my table too.[19]

Kirkconnell's preface to the book states: "This book seeks to reveal to English-speaking Canadians a transient but intensely significant phase of our national literature." The poems translated were all written during the first thirty-five years of the century and constitute a major literary step in the development of multiculturalism. Kirkconnell himself suggested that "it should help to develop in succeeding generations a Canadianism nourished by pride in the individual's past. There is nothing so shallow and sterile as the man who denies his ancestry."[20]

Kirkconnell closed the preface with the words: "It is the modest purpose of this present volume, by revealing to English-speaking Canada that these cultural traditions have already had vital expression in Canadian poetry, to press for a wider conception of national life and national literature."[21]

One result of the publication of *Canadian Overtones* was an invitation from A.S.P. Woodhouse to contribute an annual review of new Canadian letters to the *University of Toronto Quarterly*. Beginning in 1937, Kirkconnell reviewed an average of seventy books a year for the *Quarterly*, giving up this demanding task in 1966 after twenty-nine years of continuous reviewing activity.

In 1940 the federal government formed a "Nationalities Branch" — a forerunner of the Canadian Citizenship Bureau — and asked Kirkconnell to assist in its organization. He was later offered the position of director of the branch, but declined the invitation. He gave as the reason for his rejection of the offer the academic responsibilities he had just accepted as head of the Department of English at McMaster University, but the deeper reason, not voiced at the time, was that an appointment in the public service would limit his freedom of speech. In his words: "I foresaw that I could probably guard the rights and welfare of New Canadians much better as a free agent."[22]

In 1941 the director of Public Information in Ottawa issued under the authority of the minister of National War Services a forty-eight page, illustrated booklet by Kirkconnell entitled *Canadians All: A Primer of Canadian National Unity*. In the foreword, the director of Public Information states: "In this booklet, the authoritative pen of Prof. Watson Kirkconnell tells the story of the peoples of Canada, and points to a road for us to follow toward permanent unification of all our groups into one strong, resolute nation."

Kirkconnell noted that 98 percent of all Canadians in 1941 were, or were descended from, "transplanted Europeans" and went on to identify the various immigrant groups with a comment on each and the contribution it was making to Canadian society. After condemning totalitarianism and praising the type of government which allows free speech and differences of opinion, Kirkconnell stated:

The thing that unites a people into singleness of nationhood is sharing together in great common experiences, working and striving together in great common causes. Destiny has provided us with such an issue today. Out of the world's tragic errors and the black ambitions of wicked men, a monster of hate and horror has been let loose on the world; and it is our peerless privilege to stand by the side of Great Britain in withstanding and overcoming the evil creature.[23]

Despite Kirkconnell's tremendously varied achievements, I would repeat the assertion made earlier that the contribution to Canadian society and higher education which takes pride of place is his role as one of the fathers of multiculturalism. This is how one of his outstanding pupils, Dr C.H. Andrusyshen, put it in 1975: "Dr Kirkconnell was the foremost Canadian who in the thirties of the present century succeeded in effecting the beginnings of mutual concord between his own national kind and those who sought refuge in Canada from the miseries they suffered in Central and Eastern Europe."[24]

It may be that Kirkconnell himself had concluded, even by 1967, that this was to be the major contribution among all his interests and efforts. In his autobiography he wrote: "Perhaps the one thing for which I shall be remembered a century hence will be that single-handed I discovered, surveyed, and recorded in Canada's cultural Registry of Deeds this diverse collectivity of literary achievement, revealing as it does a major factor in the life of the New World."[25]

In 1936, Watson Kirkconnell, at the early age of forty-one, became a Fellow of the Royal Society of Canada. His name had not been listed on the ballots, but the Fellows elected him by a write-in, thus underlining the scholarly eminence he had achieved during his years in Winnipeg. The Royal Society was to be the vehicle through which he made what I would judge to be his second major contribution to Canadian society and higher education.

The year 1942 was a dark one for the allied nations involved in the Second World War. As yet there had been no significant victories to lighten the gloom. The Japanese attack in December 1941 on the American fleet anchored at Pearl Harbor had brought the United States into the war, but it was to be many months before the tide would turn against Germany and Japan. In Canada the war was having a positive effect on the economy, providing new jobs and increasing demands for war materials of many kinds; however, it was also having a negative effect on the lives of many people as the casualty lists lengthened, particularly of those involved in aerial warfare or the transporting of war material from Canada to Britain. The desire to promote the allied cause and increase the war effort produced many curious side effects. None was stranger than the proposal, advanced in the fall of 1942, to close the faculties of arts, commerce, education and law in all Canadian universities until the end of hostilities. There was some evidence that public opinion might support such closures and it was rumoured that Prime Minister Mackenzie King was prepared to approve it.

There was near panic among the humanities professoriate, who felt the more vulnerable when they realized that certain other disciplines had come together in 1940 to form the Canadian Social Sciences Research Council — a body that was able to mount an effective lobby at the federal level. It was Kirkconnell and some of his colleagues from Section II of the Royal Society (humanities and social sciences) who took up the matter on behalf of the threatened humanities departments. A small group met at Kirkconnell's home in Hamilton to discuss strategy. They prepared a draft document which Kirkconnell then sent to heads of humanities departments and certain university presidents. Comments and proposals for amendments were invited and a revised document was prepared and sent to the prime minister late in 1942. The statement was a comprehensive one and informed the prime minister that already almost all the students in honours and graduate courses in departments of English, classics, modern languages, and philosophy were women, or men "who are ineligible, through youth or infirmity, for military service."

The memorial went on: "We recognize that the manpower needs of the nation at war are of paramount validity, and that no fit student of draft age has any inherent right to exemption."

The document argued the case for maintaining viable humanities departments both in terms of planning for the future and even in meeting wartime needs; it records the view that: "Arts students have proved to be excellent officer material and are often better equipped to handle problems of personnel than are technically trained men."

But the main thrust of the document was not the importance of the humanities in wartime, but their intrinsic value as a component in post-war education:

In urging this maintenance of strong staffs in these departments, we are thinking in the perspective of civilization itself. Implicit in the foregoing recommendations is the conviction that the humanities are profoundly important in any long-range view of higher education. If the civilized values of the race are to survive, we shall need to have at least a fair number of men in our communities who have a strong grasp of principles, and whose minds, while appreciating practical details, can rise above these details to a sense of broad, human significance.[26]

By the spring of 1943 it had become clear that the proposed closures would not take place, but, in Kirkconnell's words: "All in all, scholars of Canada had had a bad scare", and the Royal Society decided, when it met in May in Hamilton, to appoint a committee "to consider the desirability of organizing a Humanities Research Council in Canada." Kirkconnell was appointed chairman and Milton Buchanan and Arthur Woodhouse, both from the University of Toronto, became members. The former was described by Kirkconnell as: "the scholarly, well-groomed and somewhat pessimistic professor of Spanish" and the latter as "a double for Dr Samuel Johnson in bulk, forthrightness and intellectual gusto." Kirkconnell was asked to draft a constitution and a statement of aims, and an organizational meeting took place in Hart House, University of Toronto on 29 December 1943. On that historic occasion, the Humanities

Research Council of Canada (HRCC) was formed, a sixteen-member council selected, and a five-member executive chosen. Kirkconnell was appointed as chairman of the council.

The executive committee quickly began work to form two committees to deal with grants for scholars, one dealing with research, the other with publications. This was fine, except that there was no money to disperse and the small resources that were available for the new council were provided by the Canadian Social Sciences Research Council.

Kirkconnell then led a delegation to the United States, partly to obtain information on how grants for research and publication in the humanities were handled in that country and partly to solicit from the Rockefeller Foundation funds for the HRCC. The attempt to secure funds was unsuccessful and the Canadians then visited the secretary of the Carnegie Corporation. Kirkconnell's description of this visit is worth repetition. The visitors received from Dr Lester

only a genial lecture on the sad fate, in his opinion, of all foundation-supported organizations. They began, he explained, with a paid Secretary; then added a stenographer and an office; and then the expense of a periodical of some sort. The Secretary next acquired a wife and a baby. No other sources of support were sought out, and when, after five years or ten, the Carnegie Corporation withdrew its grant, the organization folded up, and four unhappy people found themselves on the street. He was unwilling to cause all this grief to four innocent Canadians, and dismissed us with urbane cheerfulness.[27]

Kirkconnell was stung by this somewhat gloomy prognosis and resolved that it should not happen that way in Canada. He wrote to the Rockefeller Foundation, asking for money to finance a thorough survey of the humanities in Canada and to run the new council for two years while the survey took place. The letter brought results to the extent of a grant of $8,000 for the stated purposes.

The survey was extensive and thorough. The country was divided into three regions: western Canada, Ontario, and the east; the francophone institutions were treated as a fourth group, regardless of their location. Five sets of questionnaires were prepared and distributed. They were sent to university and college presidents, deans or registrars, heads of department, librarians, and each faculty member in the humanities. Visits were then made to each institution, after which sections of the report were drafted by individuals or small groups, reviewed in detail by the whole council and then sent, in the fall of 1946, to a very large number of individual administrators and scholars. Reactions and comments were received and studied, then reviewed by the full council, and a final text agreed.

In 1947 the report appeared in book form. It was a substantial volume of 209 pages, plus 78 pages of appendices. Under the title *The Humanities in Canada*, the book sold for the surprisingly low price of $2.00. The chapter entitled "Immediate Recommendations" was seven pages long and written by Kirkconnell. The whole process had been a complex and at times a tedious one and he had borne the major responsibility in connection with publication. Thirty years later, he commented: "I was never more thankful to see the end of a book."[28]

The survey and publication of the report had an interesting and important sequel. Almost all the universities made donations to the new council, a point noted with appreciation by the American foundations which received copies of *The Humanities in Canada*. The contribution of money by institutions, most of which were in difficult financial circumstances, indicated that they were serious about the maintenance and development of studies in the humanities.

For the next eleven years the Rockefeller Foundation provided the Humanities Research Council of Canada with a total of $115,000 and the Carnegie Foundation, now apparently convinced that no wives and babies would eventually be deprived because of its initial generosity, donated $80,000.

Thus the HRCC came into being as an organization with clear objectives, possessed of an extensive bank of relevant information, and led by the outstanding literary, linguistic, and philosophical figures of the day. These characteristics were of immense value in the immediate post-war years. In 1957, as a result of the major recommendation of the Massey Report, the government established the Canada Council to encourage study and enjoyment of the arts, humanities and social sciences, and to encourage the production of works of art of all kinds.

In 1977, Parliament passed the legislation which created the Social Sciences and Humanities Research Council of Canada. In order to avoid confusion with the newly created body, the Humanities

Research Council of Canada changed its name to the Canadian Federation for the Humanities (CFH). In 1983, the CFH published a very brief history of its activities and provided information concerning the creation of its parent, the Humanities Research Council of Canada.[29] It is appropriate that the name of Watson Kirkconnell occurs in the very first line of the history and that his name, along with that of A.S.P. Woodhouse, frequently occurs in the early part of the document. The history provides a brief but perceptive comment on the volume which resulted from the extensive inquiries undertaken by Kirkconnell and his colleagues.

The Humanities in Canada, written in the years leading to the Cold War, defined the pre-eminent national and international task as the replacement of ignorance and brutality by knowledge, perception, taste and morality. In a world which had become small, the authors noted the need for an intimate knowledge of different peoples and civilizations, not only for the sake of mutual survival but also for the enrichment of cultural values. Their manifesto concluded with an exhortation of humanists to play simultaneously the roles of teachers, philosophers, researchers, and artists.[30]

Kirkconnell's contribution to the formation of the HRCC was a significant one, but at the time it was not possible to see its full implication. The council came into being as a result of a wartime suggestion that departments of humanities be closed. During the 1950s, there was a sudden shift of emphasis towards scientific learning and the existence and work of the HRCC was a steadying influence. During the 1980s there has been great financial pressure on universities to reduce or eliminate certain departments; again the presence and advocacy of the council has been valuable. At present, enrolments in the humanities appear to be increasing in all parts of the country. But change is the characteristic of this decade and university planners must demonstrate, above all, flexibility in the face of changing needs. In such a situation, the CFH continues to play a crucial role.

Kirkconnell himself once wrote:

Machinery is not an inevitable cause for satisfaction. If it becomes a mere end in itself, it can be a menace to intellectual and spiritual growth. It is my own feeling, however, that all this organization of the humanities for which a few of us laid the foundations in 1942-47 has had a profound influence on these disciplines in Canada and that its greatest achievements are still to come.[31]

Few will wish to dispute any part of that statement.

Kirkconnell's first major contribution to Canadian society and higher education came about as the result of a personal project designed to provide challenge and healing when he was bereaved while a young professor at Wesley College in Winnipeg. The second, in my judgment, was made when he was an established teacher and researcher at McMaster University in Hamilton. His third contribution was made when he was president of Acadia University in Wolfville and relates to the matter of financial support by the provincial government for the universities in Nova Scotia.

When Kirkconnell was appointed as the ninth president of Acadia in 1948, he quickly discovered that one of his major problems was money, or lack of it. In 1946, the return of the veterans of the Second World War had swelled enrolment to an all-time high of 930; in 1948, there were 818 registrants and numbers steadily declined to a low of 480 in 1951. In 1948 the faculty salary scale was the lowest in Canada. As the last ex-servicemen passed through the university, so the revenues supplied by the Department of Veterans' Affairs ceased. In terms of raising replacement income, Kirkconnell was at a disadvantage. He was not a maritimer, had no base of acquaintances in the churches, and did not like fund raising, although he was willing to do out of a sense of duty what he would not have done by choice. There was a special kind of frustration arising from the fact that the Baptist Convention as a corporate entity controlled the university from the legal and administrative point of view, but provided less than 1 percent of its income, a state of affairs that necessitated a great deal of direct contact with the churches.

Kirkconnell quickly recognized that a new source of substantial funding had to be found. He believed that Nova Scotians would increasingly recognize the importance of a university education, resulting in increased enrolment, but that student fees alone would never generate enough money to effect the many changes he wished to see at Acadia. His solution to the problem lay with the provincial government. He was convinced that at least some of the costs of university education should be borne by the taxpayer. But he also understood that only a joint approach from all the institutions was likely to get a sympathetic hearing from the government. As a result of a great deal of diplomacy and quiet insistence, Kirkconnell persuaded the university presidents to move away from the intense rivalries and competition which normally prevailed to cooperate in a submission to the provincial government. He wrote the first draft of the document to be presented and led the delegation of six other presidents to meet with the Cabinet. The result was highly significant for the future of Nova Scotia universities on two counts — first, a government grant of $250,000 was approved for the institutions for the fiscal year 1958-9; second, a formula was provided for the division of the money. The formula was that each full time non-theological student in the second or subsequent year of study counted as one unit. Candidates for MA, MSc, and PhD degrees counted for three units. The allocation was to be made on the basis of weighted enrolment statistics. Kirkconnell recorded his response to the grant in these words: "The help was enthusiastically received, yet in the light of exploding registrations and exploding costs the grant was only one lambchop to seven starving tigers."[32]

When the presidents went back two years later to Premier Robert Stanfield, he decided to appoint a University Grants Commission to conduct a comprehensive study of the funding of higher education in Nova Scotia, but the key precedent had already been established that the province's universities, most of them theoretically church controlled, but certainly not church funded, were legitimate charges on the public purse.

Kirkconnell was due to retire in the summer of 1964, soon after his sixty-ninth birthday. In February of that year he suffered a serious heart attack and was forced to endure three weeks of total immobility in the Eastern Kings Memorial Hospital in Wolfville under the care of Dr Douglas Denton, the consultant cardiologist. Within two months of the attack he was back at work, preparing to leave office and writing a speech he was to deliver at Saint Mary's University in Halifax on 4 May, when he was to receive the degree of Doctor of Civil Law *honoris causa*.

It seems obvious that Kirkconnell had grown increasingly concerned over the financial situation of Acadia during the previous ten years and had decided to make his last major public speech as president a challenge to the provincial government. Parts of the speech contained sentiments and phrases ideally suited for use in the public press.

The speech began with a slightly self-derogatory image: "When a tired old racehorse is just about ready to be turned out to pasture, men may pat him on the nose, braid ribbons in his mane, feed him a few lumps of sugar and tell him what a good runner he used to be."[33] But the real theme of the speech quickly emerged and may be summed up in a single short sentence: "the universities are underfunded." By this time the young people whose birth had been termed the post-war "baby boom" were entering university and there were simply not enough resources to meet the need. The annual grant of $250,000 was gratefully acknowledged but the "lambchop to a starving tiger" image was evoked to underline its inadequacy. After deploring the high student fees and the low professorial salaries, Kirkconnell launched into the paragraph destined to provide newsworthy copy for the waiting journalists:

If, as is the case in most countries, the Government of Nova Scotia a century ago had assumed full responsibility for higher education, it would long since have supplied the necessary buildings and most of the operating revenue. Instead of this, it is private generosity that has supplied the Province with university buildings worth at least $50,000,000 and has built up professorial staffs of high competence. But if the people of Nova Scotia wish higher educational facilities to continue to be available ten years hence we shall need another $50,000,000 worth of new buildings and operating grants from the Province totalling upwards of $10,000,000 a year. Failing this, our universities are likely to become academic slums, with accommodation and staffs for only one-half of those who wish for college training. The tide of new knowledge and the tide of increased population will run together and will drown us all.

Kirkconnell expressed appreciation of the work done by Premier Stanfield and the newly formed University Grants Committee, but went on to make some pointed remarks about priorities: "If the grass-roots public still feels that paved highways on back roads are more important than the higher education of their young people, how will the money be available for this latter urgent task?"

Kirkconnell's own answer to the question was a dramatic one, no doubt deliberately designed to attract the attention of the media and the government.

There is an alternative. If the Provincial Treasurer fails to supply the funds necessary for our expansion and survival, all of the Province's universities could agree to a simultaneous increase in tuition fees to $1,500 per student or three times the rate for college students anywhere else in Canada. They would then explain to the taxpayer through a large scale press and radio campaign that it was the lack of tax dollars for higher education that compelled these desperate measures. It may be that no other solution lies ahead.

One may safely assume that a reference to capital expenditures in the amount of $50 million and annual operating grants approaching $10 million would be quoted in the press and noted by provincial politicians. The phrase "academic slums" was probably deliberately chosen to ensure quotation, and if anything could be relied on to orchestrate a chorus of protest from a united choir of students, parents, and opposition members, it would be a proposal to triple the cost of university tuition.

The *Chronicle-Herald*, Nova Scotia's provincial daily newspaper, on 5 May 1964 printed a front page report of the Convocation address and, on the following day, a cartoon by Chambers depicted Premier Stanfield, laden with honours, descending the steps of a Trans-Canada Airlines aircraft. At the foot of the steps stood Watson Kirkconnell in academic regalia, reading from a script on which certain words are clear:

...and without Provincial operating grants of $10,000,000 our universities are likely to become academic slums...

The cartoon caption was "Better Be Ready To Grab Him While He's Flush With Success."[34]

It is not possible to provide a precise description of the impact of Kirkconnell's speech at Saint Mary's University, but the publicity it received focused attention on the urgent needs of the post-secondary institutions and moved the issue firmly into the political arena.

In the case of Acadia, other events took place which directly affected the funding of the university. I refer to the secularization process, which began in 1965 and culminated in 1968. The main actors in that particular drama were the Baptist Convention, the Acadia Board of Governors, the Associated Alumni of Acadia, and the provincial government. While the key issue in the dispute was the jurisdiction of the Convention over the university, a closely related topic was that of funding. There can be no doubt of the central role played by Kirkconnell in bringing together the university presidents and then gaining the attention of the Cabinet. While others moved onto the stage as the passionate and at times bitter drama unfolded, it was largely through Kirkconnell's efforts that the precedent of provincial public money for the universities had been established in Nova Scotia. The benefits which he helped to secure were not only for Acadia; from the beginning of his campaign he had all the universities of Nova Scotia in mind.

To sum up, Kirkconnell's contribution to higher education in Canada may be encapsulated in the statement that he is the father of Canadian multiculturalism, the architect of the Humanities Research Council of Canada, and the leader of the Nova Scotia presidents in their campaign for provincial grants for the universities. His life was long, industrious, and influential in many other ways, but these activities I would list as his most important contributions. As I indicated earlier, his Baptist upbringing probably supplied the framework for his thinking about the New Canadians, and accounts, at least in part, for the high regard he had for education.[35] He not only made the most of his own unique talents, but wanted to ensure that others were given the opportunity to fulfil their potential.

Almost as a footnote to the above, we should note that Kirkconnell was, in the best sense of the word, a reactive person. Wherever he was, he would react to the challenge of any new threat or opportunity and bring his talents to bear on the situation. Not only is this illustrated by the three areas we have discussed, but by his work on behalf of the Association of Universities and Colleges of Canada, the Association of Commonwealth Universities, the Canadian Baptist Federation, the Writers' War Committee, and many other organizations. Some leaders make major contributions by imposing their questions and their answers on the constituency; others operate by responding to questions raised by the situation in which they find themselves. Kirkconnell belongs in the latter group and higher education in Canada is richer because of that fact.

Many centuries ago, when an ancient Hebrew storyteller looked back on an even more ancient time and considered the facts and legends relating to his ancestors, he made the admiring and succinct comment: "There were giants in the earth in those days."

When a contemporary academic who works in the field of language or literature, or history, or economics, or botany, or administration, looks back fifty years and sees a predecessor who excelled in all of these areas, he is inclined admiringly, but also somewhat despairingly, to echo the words of Genesis 6:4 — "There were giants in the earth in those days" — and to add that one of them was named Watson Kirkconnell.

Contributors

W.E.W. Ellis is minister of
the Fairview Baptist Church
Vancouver, British Columbia

Barry M. Moody is associate professor,
Department of History
Acadia University

J.R.C. Perkin is president
of Acadia University

G.A. Rawlyk is professor of history,
Queen's University

Notes

INTRODUCTION

1 Quoted in C.M. Johnston, *McMaster University: The Toronto Years*, 2 vols. (Toronto: University of Toronto Press, 1976), 1:35.
2 See my recently published article. "Fundamentalism, Modernism and the Maritime Baptists in the 1920s and 1930s," *Acadiensis* 17 (Autumn, 1987): 3–35.
3 Public Archives of Nova Scotia, "Records of the Church of Jebogue in Yarmouth," 140.
4 *Gospel Light*, October 1934.
5 See the discussion of this theme in Rawlyk, "Fundamentalism" 16–23.
6 W. Kirkconnell, *A Slice of Canada* (Toronto: University of Toronto Press, 1967), 148–71.
7 Quoted in ibid., 168.
8 See W. Kirkconnell, ed., *The Acadia Record, 1838–1953* (Kentville, NS: Kentville Publishing Company, 1953), 43.
9 T.J. Jackson Lears, *No Place of Grace: Antimodernism and the Transformation of American Culture 1880–1920* (New York: Random House, 1981), xvii.

CHAPTER ONE

1 Quoted in *Jubilee of Acadia College, and Memorial Exercises* (Halifax, NS: Holloway Brothers, 1889), 7.
2 Ibid.
3 Ibid., 39.
4 Ibid., 42.

5 "Memorial Address," ibid., 57–8. Saunders in his "Semi-Centennial Sermon," ibid., 28–43, develops a similar theme. See also E.A. Crawley, "The Rise and Progress of Higher Education in Connection with the Baptist Denomination in the Maritime Provinces" and Albert Coldwell, "History of Acadia College: The Vaughan Prize Essay," in *Memorials of Acadia College and Horton Academy for the Half-Century 1828–1878* (Montreal, 1881) for earlier versions of the same idea.

6 See Hilda Neatby, *Queen's University 1841–1917*, 2 vols., Frederick W. Gibson and Roger Graham, eds. (Montreal: McGill-Queen's University Press, 1978), 1:11–32; D.C. Masters, *Bishop's University* (Toronto: University of Toronto Press, 1959), 9–17; D.C. Harvey, *An Introduction to the History of Dalhousie University* (Halifax: McCurdy Printing, 1938), 9–46; Stanley B. Frost, *McGill University: For the Advancement of Learning*, 2 vols. (Montreal: McGill-Queen's University Press, 1980), 1:1–83; *The University of New Brunswick Memorial Volume*, A.G. Bailey, ed. (Fredericton: University of New Brunswick, 1950), 16–21; F.W. Vroom, *King's College: A Chronicle 1789–1939* (Halifax: Imperial Publishing Company, 1939), 10–23.

7 *Christian Messenger*, 7 July 1843, 214.

8 *A Directory of the Members of the Legislative Assembly of Nova Scotia 1758–1958*, C.B. Fergusson, ed. (Halifax, 1958), 96,284; A.W.H. Eaton, *The History of Kings County* (Belleville, Ont.: Mika, 1972), 494–5, 518–19, 685, 785; *Dictionary of Canadian Biography* (hereafter DCB). (Toronto: University of Toronto Press, 1965–), 8:709–10.

9 *Directory of MLAs*, 30–1; Eaton, *Kings County*, 569, 664, 691; I.E. Bill, *Fifty Years with the Baptist Ministers and Churches of the Maritime Provinces of Canada* (Saint John, NB: Barnes and Company, 1880), 319–20, 743–4; Acadia University Archives (hereafter AUA), Wolfville, NS, minutes of the Board of Governors, Acadia College, vol. 1.

10 DCB 10:383–8; R.S. Longley, *Acadia University, 1838–1938* (Wolfville, NS, 1939), 15–18; AUA, minutes of the Nova Scotia Baptist Education Society; B. Moody, "Joseph Howe, The Baptists and the 'College Question'" in Wayne A. Hunt, *The Proceedings of the Joseph Howe Symposium* (Halifax: Nimbus, 1984), 53–70.

11 DCB 11:214–15; ibid., forthcoming; article on John Pryor; Longley, *Acadia*, 15–65, 70–3.

12 Longley, *Acadia*, 39–41, 45–8; Bill, *Fifty Years*, 736–8; The *Christian Messenger* from 1841 until Chipman's death in June 1852, is filled with accounts of the restless energy of this remarkable man.

13 DCB 8:610–14; Eaton, *Kings County*, 310–17, 106–8; Bill, *Fifty Years*, 129–60; B. Moody, "From Itinerant to Settled Pastor; The Case of Edward Manning (1767–1851)," in Canadian Society of Church History, *Papers* (Montreal, 1981), 1–25.

14 See the various catalogues, Acadia College, from the 1860s to 1900 for the erratic story of training in theology at Acadia. Many references in the *Christian Messenger* for this same time period reveal the difficulty of raising money for this purpose from the Baptist churches of the maritimes, e.g., 28 April 1858, 131; 5 December 1860, 386; 15 July 1863, 218.

15 B. Moody, "The Founding of Acadia College: The Halifax Connection," unpublished paper delivered at the Atlantic Canada Studies Conference, Dalhousie University, 1982. Between the fall of 1838 and the spring of 1839, the *Christian Messenger* has numerous letters and articles expressing such concern. See also "Petition of the Executive Committee of the Education Society for a College Charter" (1839), reprinted in Appendix B, *Memorials of Acadia*, 246–50.

16 Longley, *Acadia*, 30–41; "Petition of the Executive Committee (1839)"; AUA, minutes of the Executive of the Nova Scotia Baptist Education Society.

17 Ibid.; DCB, 10:383–8; 11:214–15; Harvey, *Dalhousie University*, 49–51.

18 See AUA, minutes of Board of Governors, vol. 1, for numerous examples.

19 *Christian Messenger*, 28 April 1858, 131; 15 July 1863, 218.

20 See the protracted correspondence in the *Christian Messenger*, 1883.

21 Direct criticism by Convention surfaces frequently in the minutes of the Board of Governors in the twentieth century, particularly in the late 1920s and again in the 1950s. This culminated in the confrontation between Convention and board in 1965 which led to the changes in control of the university.

22 The full act, passed 27 March 1840, is reprinted in Longley, *Acadia*, appendix III, 149–51.

23 At the time of the 1965 crisis in the relationship between Convention and university, brought on by a resolution of Convention calling for a Christian faculty at Acadia, this part of the original charter was appealed to in order to show that the founders had specifically forbidden any such restrictions on faculty — *no religious tests*. See Watson Kirkconnell, *A Slice of Canada* (Toronto: University of Toronto Press, 1967), 168–70.

24 AUA, box 68, memorandum to be sent to England [1839].

25 *Christian Messenger*, 3 March 1848, 67.

26 AUA, box 68, Acadia College, [John Pryor] to __, 15 July 1878.

27 *Christian Messenger*, 11 February 1863, 42, J.M. Cramp to ed., 7 February 1863.

28 Ibid., 25 February 1874, 58.

29 Ibid., 18 March 1874, 81, Acier to ed.

30 For the development of the Acadia curriculum in the nineteenth century, see Longley, *Acadia*, 38–43, 66–103. The early course of study at the college is outlined in the *Christian Messenger*, 19 March 1841, 85, and the subsequent changes in the catalogues of the college published regularly after the early 1860s.

31 *Christian Messenger*, 4 November 1868, 363.

32 By mid-century, in the Baptist heartland of the Annapolis Valley in Nova Scotia and the Saint John River Valley, Baptists constituted close to or more than 50 per cent of the population.

33 AUA, diary of Edward Manning, 1826.

34 B. Moody, "The Maritime Baptists and Higher Education in the Early Nineteenth Century," in B. Moody, ed., *Repent and Believe; The Baptist Experience in Atlantic Canada* (Hantsport, NS: Lancelot Press, 1980), 88–102.

35 Longley, *Acadia*, 32–7.

36 Ibid., 49–58; Moody, "Howe, the Baptists…"

37 *Christian Messenger*, 20 October 1843, 333, Jane Guthrie Upham to ed.

38 Ibid., 8 July 1857, 202.

39 Ibid., 6 June 1866, 178.

40 Ibid., 12 March 1841, 74.

41 Neatby, *Queen's*, 1:151–91; Frost, *McGill*, 1:172–295.

42 DCB 12:forthcoming biography of John Pryor; Philip G.A. Allwood, "'Joseph Howe is their Devil': Controversies among Regular Baptists in Halifax, 1827–1868," in Moody, ed., *Repent and Believe*, 85–6.

43 DCB 11:209–10; T.A. Higgins, *The Life of John Mockett Cramp, D.D., 1796–1881* (Montreal: W. Drysdale & Co., 1887); AUA, J.M. Cramp, journal (typescript).

44 AUA, minutes of the Board of Governors, vol. 1, for 1852–3.

45 DCB 11:214–15; AUA, minutes of the Board of Governors, vol. I, 1853–6. The fascinating story of the mining stock speculation which carried away the personal fortunes of a number of prominent maritime Baptists, including Crawley, as well as part of Acadia's endowment fund, has not yet been fully told, although it is briefly recounted in Longley, *Acadia*, 72. A more complete picture can be pieced together from AUA, letterbook of the West Columbia Mining and Manufacturing Company, and minutes

of the Board of Governors, vol. I, 1853–60. Novelist James B. DeMille, secretary of the company for a brief period, later fictionalized the story as the *Minnehaha Mines*, serialized in *New Dominion and True Humorist*, 1870.

46 Longley, *Acadia*, 82–103; AUA, minutes of the Board of Governors, vol. 11, 1869–96.

47 *Christian Messenger*, 4 November 1857, 339; 14 April 1858, 117.

48 See Frost, *McGill*, 1:83, 102, 110, 116–20; Neatby, *Queen's*, 111, 134–6; Vroom, *King's*, 37.

49 Longley, *Acadia*, 39–41, 45–8, 69–70; Bill, *Fifty Years*, 736–8; *Christian Messenger*, June and July 1852, for accounts of Chipman's death and evaluations of his significance to the denomination and the college.

50 Ibid., 29 April 1863, 129–30.

51 A.B. McKillop, *A Disciplined Intelligence: Critical Inquiry and Canadian Thought in the Victorian Era* (Montreal: McGill-Queen's University Press, 1979), 119; Ramsay Cook, *The Regenerators; Social Criticism in Late Victorian English Canada* (Toronto: University of Toronto Press, 1985), 20.

52 *The Acadia Record* (Kentville, NS, 1953), 4.

53 McKillop, *Disciplined Intelligence*, 29.

54 An examination of the courses and the required texts clearly demonstrates the presence of such key influences as Wayland and Paley. See *Christian Messenger*, 19 March 1841, 85, and catalogues of the college, 1863 onward.

55 *Christian Messenger*, 24 August 1838, 268.

56 Allison A. Trites, "The New Brunswick Seminary, 1836–1895," in Moody, *Repent and Believe*, 103–7.

57 *Christian Messenger*, 16 March 1849, 81, ABCD to ed.

58 Ibid., 28 December 1849, 411; 9 January 1856, 13–4; 23 July 1856, 238; 9 July 1856, 222; 27 February 1861, 70; 21 November 1860, 371; 5 December 1860, 386; James Davison, *Alice of Grand Pré* (Wolfville, NS: Lancelot Press, 1981), 33–70.

59 *Christian Messenger*, 9 July 1856, 222.

60 Ibid., 27 February 1856, 65–6.

61 Ibid., 14 August 1858, 262, A Father to ed.

62 Margaret Gillett, *We Walked Very Warily: A History of Women at McGill* (Montreal: Eden Press, 1981), chapters 1–4.

63 AUA, minutes of the Board of Governors, vol. I: 210, minute of 3 June 1874.

64 *The Baptist Year Book, of the Maritime Provinces of Canada* (Halifax: Messenger Printing Office, 1881), 28.

65 Ibid., xl.

66 See McKillop, *Disciplined Intelligence*; Cook, *The Regenerators*; and Carl Berger, *Science, God, and Nature in Victorian Canada* (Toronto: University of Toronto Press, 1983), for fuller discussion of Canadian response to these problems.

67 *Christian Messenger*, 19 May 1848, 158–9, Obed Chute to ed.

68 Ibid., 9 January 1856, 10.

69 Ibid., 12 June 1867, 186–7, J.M. Cramp's address to the graduating class.

70 See McKillop, *Disciplined Intelligence*, 186–7; Cook, *The Regenerators*, 15.

71 *Christian Messenger*, 6 July 1870, 209–10, graduating essay of W.H. Newcomb, "The Problem of Life." See also ibid., 17 June 1881, 189, oration by G.F. Currie, "Tendencies of Modern Scientific Inquiry."

72 Ibid., 27 July 1870, 233–4, William Elder to ed.

73 Ibid., 24 January 1845, 25.

74 Ibid., 2 September 1874, 274–5, report to Convention by E.W. Sawyer.

75 Ibid., 21 September 1870, 298.

CHAPTER TWO

1 C. Johnston, *McMaster University: The Toronto Years*, 2 vols. (Toronto: University of Toronto Press, 1976), 1:3.

2 Ibid., 19.

3 W.S. Fox, ed., *Letters of William Davies, Toronto, 1854–1861* (Toronto: University of Toronto Press, 1945), 112.

4 See the confidential letter from N.W. Rowell to Chancellor H.P. Whidden, 30 May 1928, in the Whidden papers, Canadian Baptist Archives, McMaster Divinity College, Hamilton, Ontario. Hereafter the abbreviation for the archives will be CBA.

5 Ibid.

6 Ibid.

7 Johnston, *McMaster University*, I:30.

8 T.J. Jackson Lears, "The Concept of Cultural Hegemony: Problems and Possibilities," *American Historical Review* 90, no. 3 (June 1985): 568.

9 T. Harpur, *For Christ's Sake* (Toronto: McClelland and Stewart, 1986), 53. I am indebted to Mrs Doris Odell for this quotation as well as the previous one.

10 See A. Gramsci, *Selections from the Prison Notebooks* (New York: International Publications Company, 1971). This quotation is from P. Craven, *'An Impartial Umpire': Industrial Relations and the Canadian State 1900–1911* (Toronto: University of Toronto Press, 1981), 15.

11 See N.K. Clifford, "His Dominion: A Vision in Crisis," *Studies in Religion*, ii (1973): 315–26.

12 Quoted in Craven, *"An Impartial Umpire,"* 16.

13 See R.W. Fox and T.J. Jackson Lears, eds., *The Culture of Consumption* (New York: Random House, 1983), xi.

14 Ibid., xi–xii. See also T.J. Jackson Lears' brilliant book *No Place of Grace: Antimodernism and the Transformation of American Culture 1880–1920* (New York: Random House, 1981).

15 M.E. Marty, *Modern American Religion: The Irony of It All, 1893–1919*, 4 vols. (Chicago: University of Chicago Press, 1986), 1:17–90.

16 D.W. Frank, *Less Than Conquerors: How Evangelicals Entered The Twentieth Century* (Grand Rapids: W.B. Eerdmans, 1986), 222.

17 Quoted in ibid., 222.

18 Ibid., 223.

19 Karl Marx and Friedrich Engels, *The Communist Manifesto* (New York: Washington Square Press, 1964), 63.

20 N. Furniss, *The Fundamentalist Controversy, 1918–1931* (New Haven: Yale University Press, 1954), 36.

21 See C.H. Pinnock, "The Modernist Impulse at McMaster University, 1887–1927," in J. Zeman, ed., *Baptists in Canada* (Burlington: Welch, 1980), 195.

22 W.E. Ellis, "Social and Religious Factors in the Fundamentalist-Modernist Schisms Among Baptists in North America, 1895–1934," (PhD thesis, University of Pittsburgh, 1974), 284.

23 Quoted in the Toronto *Globe*, 21 October 1925 in an article entitled "Overwhelming Vote Cast in Convention for Professor Marshall."

24 O.C.S. Wallace to S.J. Moore, 9 November 1926, Whidden papers, CBA.

25 Johnston, *McMaster University*, 1:40.

26 Rowell to Whidden, 30 May 1928, Whidden papers, CBA.

27 *Baptist Year Book*, 1883, 75.

28 See Johnston, *McMaster University*, 1:73.

29 Fox and Lears, *The Culture of Consumption*, xiii. The evolution of the theological and social views of Wallace may be seen in his popular writing in the *Canadian Baptist* and the *Maritime Baptist* in the first three decades of the twentieth century.

30 *McMaster University Monthly*, 5(1985): 100–5.

31 T.P. Hall to Wallace, 17 December 1895, Wallace papers, CBA. The quotation is to be found in Johnston, *McMaster University*, I:72.

32 The evolution of Wallace's thinking while he was chancellor, and

afterwards, was not a major concern of Johnston in his Wallace chapter. See Johnston, *McMaster University*, I:70–84.

33 Ibid., 73.

34 Minutes of the McMaster University Senate, 29 May 1909, CBA.

35 Minutes of the McMaster University Senate, 2 December 1909, CBA.

36 W.S.M. McLay to McKay, 17 May 1911, McLay Papers, CBA.

37 *Simcoe Reformer*, 15 April 1935.

38 Ibid.

39 Ibid.

40 Ibid.

41 "Baptists Facing the Future," undated, McCrimmon papers, CBA.

42 Ibid.

43 "McCrimmon Obituary," ibid., CBA.

44 *McMaster University Monthly*, February 1893.

45 McCrimmon papers, CBA.

46 See A.L. McCrimmon, *The Educational Policy of the Baptists of Ontario and Quebec* (Toronto, 1920), 9.

47 Ibid., 21.

48 Ibid., 22.

49 Ibid., 25.

50 Ibid., 31.

51 Ibid., 26.

52 Quoted in Johnston, *McMaster University*, 1:166. The quotation was originally used in the *McMaster University Alumni News* obituary of McCrimmon, written by his friend Dean McLay, 4 May 1935.

53 For McCrimmon's critique, however muted, of the new McMaster, see his "The Preservation of the Christian Character and of the Denominational Control of McMaster University," 1930, McCrimmon papers, CBA.

54 *McMaster University Alumni News*, 23 May 1952.

55 *Canadian Baptist*, 15 April 1952.

56 Fox to McMaster University Alumni Office, 1 June 1941, CBA.

57 See Ellis, "Social and Religious Factors" for the best available study on this topic.

58 Whidden's "What is a liberal education?," *Canadian Journal of Religious Thought*, 1(1924):39, is obviously a boiled down version of the 1923 inaugural address.

59 See the *Canadian Baptist*, 22 November 1923.

60 *Baptist Year Book*, 1924, 43.

61 For an almost week by week and blow by blow account of unfolding

events from a Shields' perspective, see the *Gospel Witness* for the 1924–27 period. For the Convention side, see G.W. Carder, "Controversy in the Baptist Convention, 1908–1929," (BD thesis, McMaster University 1950).

62 Quoted in J.D.E. Dozois, "Dr. Thomas Todhunter Shields (1873–1955): In the Stream of Fundamentalism," (BD thesis, McMaster Divinity College, 1963), 57.

63 *Saturday Night*, 11 July 1931.

64 G. Anglin, "The Battling Baptist," *MacLean's* 15 June 1949. I am indebted to Ms Lee Ann Purchace for some of this material about Shields.

65 C.A. Russell, "Thomas Todhunter Shields, Canadian Fundamentalist," *Ontario History*, 70(1978), 264.

66 T.T. Shields, *The Plot That Failed* (Toronto: Gospel Witness, 1937), 10.

67 Ibid., 11.

68 *Gospel Witness*, 5 October 1922.

69 Ibid.

70 Ibid., 12 October 1922.

71 Ibid., 31 May 1923.

72 Ibid., 29 November 1923.

73 Ibid., 14 February 1924.

74 Johnston, *McMaster University*, 1:180.

75 *Gospel Witness*, 23 September 1926. This important letter has not received the attention it certainly warrants.

76 Ibid.

77 Ibid.

78 Ibid.

79 Ibid., 27 August 1925.

80 Ibid.

81 Ibid., 5 November 1925.

82 L.K. Tarr, *Shields of Canada* (Grand Rapids: Baker, 1967), 99.

83 Johnston, *McMaster University*, 1:199.

84 For an excellent study of Shields and Des Moines, see G.S. May, "Des Moines University and Dr. T.T. Shields," *Iowa Journal of History* (July 1956), 193–232.

85 Johnston, *McMaster University*, 1:xii.

86 Quote in ibid., 193, from a 1926 letter from the Reverend W.A. Cameron to Whidden.

87 Quoted in ibid., 181. I am far less sympathetic to Whidden than is Johnston, largely because I do not feel that the McMaster of today is the only prism through which to view the events of the 1920s. In other

words, McMaster could have become a small, reputable Christian college like Wheaton College, Illinois, rather than the large and secular science dominated institution of the 1980s. But the point still has to be made that the historian must deal with what actually happened and why and not what might have happened — *if.*

CHAPTER THREE

1 Charles M. Johnston, *McMaster University: The Toronto Years,* 2 vols. (Toronto: University of Toronto Press, 1976), 1:14.
2 Minutes of annual meetings of the Home Mission Convention of Manitoba and North-West, Red River Association and Sunday School, 28–30 June 1883, Portage La Prairie (Canadian Baptist Archives, McMaster Divinity College, hereafter CBA), 4.
3 *The Western Baptist* (hereafter WB) 31, no. 11 (1930): 4–5.
4 John E. Davis, *The Life of a Leper, Autobiography of John E. Davis, Baptist Missionary Among the Telugus* (Canadian Baptist Foreign Mission Board n.d. [1918?]), 26–34.
5 Ibid., 27.
6 *The Canadian Baptist* (hereafter CB), 3 June 1884: 4.
7 Davis, *Life of a Leper,* 33.
8 *The North-West Baptist* (hereafter NB) 1, no. 2 (1885): 4.
9 NB, 4, no. 6 (1 February 1888): 4.
10 NB, 5, no. 10 (1 May 1890): 4.
11 Walter E. Ellis, "Organizational and Educational Policy of Baptists in Western Canada 1873–1939," (BD thesis, Faculty of Divinity, McMaster University 1962): 94.
12 NB, 9, no. 8 (Fall 1893): 22.
13 NB, 5, no. 1 (1 August 1889): 6.
14 C.C. McLaurin, *Pioneering in Western Canada, a Story of the Baptists* (Calgary: Armae Press, 1939), 296–7; see also Charles G. Stone and F. Joan Garnett, *Brandon College: A History, 1899–1967* (Brandon: Brandon University, 1969).
15 Minutes, Brandon College Board, 11 July 1899, hereafter, MBCB, (Brandon University Archives, hereafter BUA).
16 Leland Clark, *Brandon's Politics and Politicians* (Brandon: Sun Press, 1981), 8–9.
17 *Annual Announcement of Brandon College* 1900–1901 (Brandon: Times Fine Book & Job Office, 1900), 11; 1901–1902, 19.

18 *NB*, 11, no. 15 (1 March 1907): 4.

19 For Baptist attempts to obtain university status see; "The University Question," *NB*, 20, no. 16 (15 March 1906): 3; "The Charter and Brandon College," ibid., 21, no. 14 (15 February 1907): 3; and, "Baptist Position on Education," *NB*, 21, no. 15 (1 March 1907): 4.

20 Minutes, Brandon College Board 11 January 1906, (hereafter MBCB), 44.

21 Johnston, *McMaster University*, 1:81.

22 McLaurin, *Pioneering in Western Canada*, 168.

23 MBCB, 6 October 1909, 74.

24 MBCB, 11 April 1909, 120–1.

25 Letter, A.P. McDiarmid to Brandon College Board, 4 September 1911, filed with MBCB, 142.

26 *The Western Outlook* (hereafter WO) 5, no. 4 (15 February 1912): 4.

27 MBCB, 16, 24 February 1912, 152–6.

28 WO, 5, no. 11 (1 June 1912): 6–10.

29 Letter, W. Sherwood Fox to J.H. Farmer, 5 March 1912, dean's correspondence, McMaster University, CBA. The critical importance of pastoral leadership is shown by the fact that population had risen from 150,000 in Alberta and Saskatchewan in 1905, to 600,000 in Saskatchewan alone by 1914. That year the Baptist Union reported 253 churches, 49 in Manitoba, 47 each in Saskatchewan and Alberta, and 49 in British Columbia. However, of these 26 in Manitoba, 30 in Saskatchewan, 27 in Alberta, and 22 in BC were mission churches. Thirty-two of the 33 German congregations were mission congregations as were all of the 25 Scandinavian congregations. They were served by 176 active pastors and denominational leaders, 33 of whom were ethnic. Pastors were desperately needed to meet congregational and population growth.

30 MBCB, 7 March 1912, 158.

31 Ibid., 159–68.

32 MBCB, 12 December 1913, 189; 15 November 1912, 169–71.

33 MBCB, 21 February 1917.

34 MBCB, 6 September 1917.

35 Stone, *Brandon College*, 85.

36 WB, 10, no. 2 (February 1917): 14.

37 Leland Clark, *Brandon's Politics and Politicians*, 80–3.

38 "Whidden's Masterly Address in Commons," *Brandon Sun*, 20 June 1919, 1, 8. In referring to labour, Whidden expressed sympathy, but seems also to have espoused the Bolshevist conspiracy theory. "Sir," he said, "there is true labor, and we should honor it and stand for its rights ... But there

is also rank, naked, unadorned Redism, and sometimes, unfortunately for true labor, this menace becomes associated with people who are honestly endeavoring to solve their problems and secure the interest of all broadminded fellow citizens in order to obtain their due."; L. Clark, *Brandon's Politics and Politicians*, 97.

39 J. Brian Scott, "Comments," *Celebrating the Canadian Baptist Heritage* (Hamilton: Hurley Press, 1984), 74.

40 Quoted in Johnston, *McMaster University*, 1:112.

41 WO, 6, no. 10 (15 May 1913): 1,4: Whidden's liberalism, like Harris L. MacNeill's, seems to have been confined to theology and education; see: H.P. Whidden, "What is a Liberal Education?" *Canadian Journal of Religious Thought* 1(1924): 39ff.

42 Chancellor's correspondence, case 3, 1897. H.P. Whidden to OCS Wallace, CBA, 2 January 1897.

43 I.C. Morgan, "Harris Lachlan MacNeill: A biographical sketch," in J.R.C. Perkin, ed., "Summer in His Soul: Essays in Honour of Harris L. MacNeill," *Theological Bulletin* (May 1969): 5–6. Scholars interested in the fundamentalist-modernist controversy among Baptists in western Canada will consult: *Report of the Brandon College Commission* (Calgary: January 1923), BUA, Acc. no. r79–54.

44 W.H.P. Faunce, "Freedom in School and Church," in *Worlds Work* 45 (March 1923): 509–11. Quoted in Johnston, *McMaster University*, 1:171.

45 WB, 16, no. 7 (August 1923): 1, 4.

46 WB, 18, no. 1 (February 1925): 5.

47 MBCB, 12 March 1924.

48 WB, 18, no. 11 (November 1925): 1, 4–5.

49 In June 1926, Chancellor Whidden of McMaster cautioned Dr MacNeill and the Brandon board against expanding courses and faculty at Brandon, but recognized it was difficult "in view of the fact that we are expanding down here to meet our needs." They should insist on "no more professors until they know how to pay for those already on the staff," he commented. Whidden to J.W. Litch, DD, Vancouver, 17 June 1926; Chancellor's correspondence, CBA. By contrast, MBCB, 9 June 1926.

50 Letter, C.H. Lager to W.E. Matthews 8 June 1926: filed with MBCB.

51 CC, 1926, CBA, H.H. Bingham to Whidden, 19 July 1926.

52 Stone, *Brandon College*, 117.

53 "Report," *Baptist Union Year Book 1928* (Winnipeg: Stovel, 1929), 66–74; WB, 22, no. 1 (March 1929): 2.

54 WB, 22, no. 9 (October 1929): 1.

55 As part of the debate over continuance of Brandon College, submissions were requested from interested Baptist constituents. See: Letter, Rev G.A. Reynolds to BCB 10 June 1931. Reynolds, pastor of Kerrisdale Baptist Church, Vancouver, held that Baptists should "give up continuing an Arts College and a cultural school for the children of the well to do people."; WB, 24, no. 2 (March 1931): 2.

56 Letter, S.J. McKee to Tarr, 27 August 1931, BCA.

57 Details of the heroic efforts to solve the financial crises of the college under depression conditions can be followed in detail in the minutes of the Brandon College Board and Executive Board. The brilliant but mercurial C.H. Lager threatened legal action against the board because the school was in default of interest. He caustically referred to the American Baptist Publication Society, which held $30,000 in bonds as the "sentimental shareholder," while he charged that simple people lost their life savings. Meanwhile the college administration pursued their agendas unconcerned. Correspondence, C.H. Lager to BCB, filed with MBCB 20 May 1932.; see also: Stone, Brandon College, 143–47.

58 W.E. Mann, Sect, Cult, and Church in Alberta (Toronto: University of Toronto Press, 1955), 117.

59 J.R.C. Evans to Brandon College Local Executive, 30 November 1937; filed with MBCB, BUA.

60 Ibid., 2.

61 Baptist Union of Western Canada Year Book 1937–38 (Edmonton: 1938), 58–9. The vexatious question of who ultimately has control of Baptist education — the Union or the Brandon College Board — surfaced as attempts were made to resolve the issue of closing the institution. See: minutes, Manitoba Section BCB, 21 March 1938.

62 Cited in Stone, Brandon College, 130.

63 History of Brandon College Inc. (Brandon: n.p. 1962), 34–41.

64 Martin Marty, The Modern Schism (New York: Harper & Row, 1969), 140.

65 Johnston, McMaster University, 1:234.

66 The Gospel Witness, 4, no. 28 (11 May 1925): 13. Dr T.T. Shields' classic phrase was, "[McMaster] imagines that the Denomination exists for McMaster — not McMaster for the Denomination."

67 Mann, Sect, Cult, and Church, 82–3.

68 Sidney E. Mead, "American Protestantism Since the Civil War," Richard M. Abrams & L.W. Levine, eds. The Shaping of Twentieth-Century America (Boston: Little Brown, 1971), 174–5.

69 Peter G. Mode, *The Frontier Spirit in American Christianity*, (New York: MacMillan, 1923).
70 Watson Kirkconnell, personal file, University of Winnipeg Archives; from an address given in the 1940s.

CHAPTER FOUR

1 The story is told on p. 55–6 of Kirkconnell's autobiography, *A Slice of Canada* (Toronto: University of Toronto Press, 1967), hereafter referred to as SC.
2 For a brief biography of Watson Kirkconnell, see J.R.C. Perkin and James Snelson, *Morning in His Heart* (Hantsport, NS: Lancelot Press, 1986) hereafter referred to as *Morning*.
3 SC, 56.
4 *European Elegies* (Ottawa: The Graphic Publishers, 1928), 102 (hereafter referred to as *Elegies*).
5 Ibid., 82.
6 Ibid., 139.
7 Copies of this correspondence are located in the Kirkconnell papers (hereafter referred to as KP) in the library at Acadia University, Wolfville, NS.
8 SC, 57.
9 KP.
10 Ibid., letter, 20 September 1926.
11 Ibid., letter, 19 July 1926.
12 For general discussion, see J.R.C. Perkin, "Kirkconnell's Methodology of Verse Translation," in *Journal of the Atlantic Provinces Linguistic Association* 5 (1983): 16–32.
13 KP, letter, 29 November 1928. One sentence in the letter reads: "I say of this Introduction: 'Stat et stet'."
14 For a discussion of the sequence whereby a personal project became a major academic achievement, which in turn established links with immigrant peoples, see N.F. Dreisziger, "Watson Kirkconnell: Translator of Hungarian Poetry and Friend of Hungarian-Canadians," in *Canadian-American Review of Hungarian Studies*, vol. 4, no. 2 (Fall 1977), particularly 125–6.
15 This comment is based largely on personal conversation with Dr Kirkconnell and a reference by Janet Kirkconnell to her father's "crusade on behalf of new Canadian education."

16 I understand that a two-volume reference work on Canadian literature in the non-official languages is in preparation and will be published by the University of Ottawa Press. An extensive introduction will recognize Kirkconnell's unique contribution to the development of multiculturalism in Canada.

17 Kirkconnell's marriage to Hope Kitchener brought life-long security and satisfaction. There were three children of this union, Helen, Janet, and Susan, all currently resident in Nova Scotia. In 1967, Kirkconnell recorded his appreciation of family life in these words: "Sometimes I think that what I prize most is my experience of a happy marriage, with its fruit in two King's Scouts and three Girl Guides, all grown up to useful maturity." (SC, 362.)

18 *Canadian Overtones* (Winnipeg: The Columbia Press, 1935), 16, hereafter referred to as *Overtones*.

19 Ibid., 58.

20 Ibid., 4.

21 Ibid., 6.

22 SC, 276.

23 *Canadians All*, 19.

24 In J.R.C. Perkin, ed., *The Undoing of Babel* (Toronto: McClelland and Stewart, 1975), 33.

25 SC, 76–7.

26 The complete text of the "Memorial on Studies in the Humanities in Canada" is given in SC, 237–9.

27 Ibid., 242.

28 Ibid., 245.

29 *The Canadian Federation for the Humanities, 1943–1983: A Short History* (Ottawa: Canadian Federation for the Humanities, 1983).

30 Ibid., 3.

31 SC, 248.

32 Ibid., 159.

33 The complete text of the speech, Kirkconnell's original copy, is among his papers in the Acadia archives.

34 In a private letter, Mr Stanfield acknowledges that he remembers the events, but does not recall what honours he had received. He believes that he was returning from a trip to Europe, during which he had called on the mayor of Paris, in which city he had made a speech entirely in French.

35 There is a fascinating section in SC in which Kirkconnell allows a rare glimpse into his views of the Baptist denomination, its ministers, and its theology. He speaks of the "primitive democracy of the Baptist congregation" and refers to it as "the most appropriate and salutary polity for a religious community." He condemns the factionalism of the Baptist clergy "fighting among themselves and usually with zeal in inverse proportion to their knowledge." This he calls "ministerial gangsterism." The paragraph which follows deals with doctrine and asserts that he had been reared in the liberal Baptist tradition which allows the believer to frame his theology in his own terms. The whole section is couched in strong language and offers a clue to many of Kirkconnell's religious attitudes.

Index